CHILD CARE AND THE GROWTH OF LOVE

John Bowlby was born in 1907 and educated at the R[illegible] Dartmouth and Trinity College, Cambridge. After medical studies at University College Hospital [illegible] psychiatry and psychoanalysis. From 1940 to 1945 [illegible] three years dealing with the selection of officers. [illegible] he worked full time at the Tavistock Clinic and the [illegible] Institute of Human Relations, his appointment latterly being [illegible] the joint auspices of the National Health Service and the [illegible] Research Council. Until 1972 he was Director of the Department [illegible] Children and Parents. He continued work at the Tavistock [illegible] role of senior research fellow and teacher after his retirement.

He was training secretary and deputy president of the [illegible] Psychoanalytical Society and president of the International [illegible] ation for Child Psychiatry and Allied Professions. In 1950 [illegible] appointed consultant in mental health to the World H[illegible] Organization, for whom he wrote *Maternal Care and Mental He[illegible]* He also wrote *Forty-Four Juvenile Thieves*, *Child Care and the G[illegible]* *Love*, his major work, *Attachment and Loss*: Volume 1, *Attachm[illegible]* Volume 2, *Separation: Anxiety and Anger* and Volume 3, *Loss: Sa[illegible]* *and Depression*, *The Making and Breaking of Affectional Bonds* and [illegible] *Secure Base*.

John Bowlby died in 1990. In his obituary, *The Times* wrote [illegible] 'enormous influence' while the *Daily Telegraph* called him 'a [illegible] ing figure in his field . . . a truly great teacher, [who] inspired [illegible] dedicated followers'.

CHILD CARE AND THE GROWTH OF LOVE

*

SECOND EDITION

BASED BY PERMISSION OF THE
WORLD HEALTH ORGANIZATION

ON THE REPORT

Maternal Care and Mental Health

BY

JOHN BOWLBY

M.A. M.D. F.R.C.P.

*

ABRIDGED AND EDITED BY

MARGERY FRY

I.L.D. D.C.L., J.P. M.A.

WITH TWO NEW CHAPTERS BY

MARY D. SALTER AINSWORTH

M.A. Ph.D

PENGUIN BOOKS

PENGUIN BOOKS

Published by the Penguin Group
Penguin Books Ltd, 27 Wrights Lane, London W8 5TZ, England
Penguin Putnam Inc., 375 Hudson Street, New York, New York 10014, USA
Penguin Books Australia Ltd, Ringwood, Victoria, Australia
Penguin Books Canada Ltd, 10 Alcorn Avenue, Toronto, Ontario, Canada M4V 3B2
Penguin Books (NZ) Ltd, 182–190 Wairau Road, Auckland 10, New Zealand

Penguin Books Ltd, Registered Offices: Harmondsworth, Middlesex, England

Published in Pelican Books 1953
Second edition 1965
Reprinted in Penguin Books 1990
5 7 9 10 8 6 4

Printed in England by Clays Ltd, St Ives plc
Set in Monotype Baskerville

Contents

PART III

Further Research into the Adverse Effects of Maternal Deprivation

Preface to First Edition

AT the third session of the Social Commission of the United Nations held in April 1948 it was decided to make a study of the needs of homeless children. These were described as 'children who are orphaned or separated from their families for other reasons and need care in foster-homes, institutions or other types of group care'. The study was to be confined to 'children who were homeless in their native country', thus explicitly excluding refugees from war or other disaster. When the specialized agencies interested in the matter were approached by the United Nations for their comments and suggestions, the World Health Organization offered to contribute a study of the mental health aspects of the problem. This offer was accepted and has resulted in the report on which this book is based.

Dr Bowlby took up temporary appointment with the World Health Organization in January 1950, and during the late winter and early spring he visited several countries in Europe – France, the Netherlands, Sweden, Switzerland, and the United Kingdom – and the United States of America. In each he had discussions with workers, most of whom were concerned with child care and child guidance, saw something of their work, and was introduced to the literature. In these discussions he found a very high degree of agreement existing both in regard to the principles underlying the mental health of children and the practices by which it may be safeguarded.

In such a report certain things are necessary. Sources of information must be given, and full recognition made of the experts whose work has been drawn upon. Statistics must be used whenever they are available and clearly presented for the use of later students. The utmost exactitude is necessary in the actual wording of the report, and this often involves the use of technical language. All these things are necessary, but they do not make such a scholarly report easy reading for the general public. The ordinary reader is apt to shy away from a page bristling with references and figures, with unfamiliar words and names which convey nothing to him. Yet the matter of this report very closely concerns the welfare of our whole society. So it has seemed worth while to produce a version of the report, abridged and to some extent simplified for general reading. This has been revised by Dr Bowlby, who has also added some paragraphs to the end of the first chapter. Serious students of the matter dealt with will not need to be warned that they must not content themselves with this simplified version but must refer back to the original report by Dr John Bowlby, *Maternal Care and Mental Health*, on which this book is based. This, published in 1951, is obtainable, direct or through a bookseller, from the World Health Organization, Geneva, from Her Majesty's Stationery Office, Kingsway, London, price 13*s* 6*d* in paper and 17*s* 6*d* bound, and from the Columbia University Press, New York, price $2.00 paper and $2.50 bound.

Permission to quote has kindly been given by the authors and publishers of the many works referred to in the text; for this we are most grateful. Bibliographical references are given on page 243.

August 1952 **S.M.F.**

Preface to Second Edition

It is now some years since this book and the original report on which it is based were published. Those years have seen keen interest in its thesis, much new evidence, and lively debate of the scientific issues raised. They have seen also an ever-widening recognition of the need to ensure that children receive the care and affection now known to be necessary for their healthy development.

Whilst the benefits of maternal care and the dangers of deprivation are now generally accepted, many aspects of the matter nevertheless remain controversial. How specific are the adverse effects? How permanent is the damage? What exactly causes it? Because these and many similar questions are asked and argued the World Health Organization decided it would be useful to look afresh at the problem; and in 1962 a collection of articles by a number of distinguished workers appeared under the title *Deprivation of Maternal Care: a Reassessment of its Effects*.* Of these articles the last and longest is by Dr Mary Salter Ainsworth, an old colleague of mine. In it she considers the views expressed by other contributors and presents a comprehensive review of the field.

Dr Salter Ainsworth's article has provided a good opportunity to prepare a new edition of this book. With the permission of the World Health Organization and the collaboration of Dr Salter Ainsworth herself the article has been used as a basis for two new chapters. The first identifies eight issues that have given rise to controversy, and the second considers how each of them looks in the light of the most recent evidence. Only trifling changes have been made to the rest of the book.

This edition ends with the same brief 'Conclusion' that appeared in the first edition. Though awareness of the

* *W H O Public Health Papers*, No. 14, Geneva (London: H.M.S.O.; New York: Columbia University Press).

problem is now sharper and in many countries great efforts are being made to improve services, a vast amount remains to be done. With only small revisions, therefore, the views I expressed in 1951 still stand. May the time when they are dated come soon.

Preparation of the two additional chapters is, alas, not by the hand of Margery Fry, who died in 1958. Since it is entirely to her enthusiasm and skill, when long past her seventieth birthday, that this shortened version of my report is due, I remain permanently and deeply in her debt.

July 1964 J. B.

Part I

ADVERSE EFFECTS OF MATERNAL DEPRIVATION

CHAPTER I

Some Causes of Mental Ill-health

AMONG the most significant developments of psychiatry* during the past quarter of a century has been the steady growth of evidence that the quality of the parental care which a child receives in his earliest years is of vital importance for his future mental health.

Largely as a result of this new knowledge, there is today a high level of agreement among child-guidance workers in Europe and America on certain central notions. These workers are alike in the way in which they approach and study and diagnose their patients, in the aims of their treatments, and above all in the theories of the causes of mental ill-health on which their work is founded. What these are will be discussed in the course of this book. For the moment it is sufficient to say that what is believed to be essential for mental health is that an infant and young child should experience a warm, intimate, and continuous relationship with his mother (or permanent mother-substitute – one person who steadily 'mothers' him) in which both find satisfaction and enjoyment. It is this complex, rich, and rewarding relationship with the mother in early years, varied in countless ways by relations with the father and with the brothers and sisters, that child psychiatrists and many others now believe to underlie the development of character and of mental health.

* Four words will be used frequently in this book and it is well to define them at the outset.

Psychology: Science of human behaviour and the human mind.

Psychologist: One who makes a study of psychology.

Psychiatry: Medical treatment of disorders of behaviour and disorders of the mind.

Psychiatrist: A qualified doctor who specializes in the treatment of disorders of behaviour and disorders of the mind.

A state of affairs in which a child does not have this relationship is termed 'maternal deprivation'. This is a general term covering a number of different situations. Thus, a child is deprived even though living at home if his mother (or permanent mother-substitute) is unable to give him the loving care small children need. Again, a child is deprived if for any reason he is removed from his mother's care. This deprivation will be relatively mild if he is then looked after by someone whom he has already learned to know and trust, but may be considerable if the foster-mother even though loving is a stranger. All these arrangements, however, give a child some satisfaction and are therefore examples of '*partial deprivation*'. They stand in contrast to the almost '*complete deprivation*' which is still not uncommon in institutions, residential nurseries, and hospitals, where a child often has no *one* person who cares for him in a personal way and with whom he may feel secure.

The ill-effects of deprivation vary with its degree. Partial deprivation brings in its train anxiety, excessive need for love, powerful feelings of revenge, and, arising from these last, guilt and depression. A young child, still immature in mind and body, cannot cope with all these emotions and drives. The ways in which he responds to these disturbances of his inner life may in the end bring about nervous disorders and instability of character. Complete deprivation, with which we shall be dealing principally in this book, has even more far-reaching effects on character development and may entirely cripple the capacity to make relationships with other people. Many workers have investigated the connexion between 'broken homes' and the failure of children to adjust themselves to life with other people. But though these studies have confirmed the far-reaching importance of a child's early experience of home, the idea of a 'broken home' brings in too many varied conditions to be a satisfactory classification for scientific study; it is better to fix our minds on the child's developing relationship with his mother and his father. When we do this, much that was obscure in the origins of mental illness becomes clear.

An illustration of the fruitfulness of this standpoint is a study of 102 persistent offenders aged between fifteen and eighteen years in an English Approved School, which showed clearly how anxieties arising from unsatisfactory relationships in early childhood predispose children to respond in an anti-social way to later stresses. Most of the early anxiety situations amongst these boys were particular aspects of maternal deprivation.

Naturally, there are many other ways besides deprivation, arising from separation or outright rejection, in which parent–child relationships may become unhealthy. The commonest are (*a*) an unconsciously rejecting attitude underlying a loving one; (*b*) an excessive demand for love and reassurance on the part of a mother; and (*c*) a mother's unconsciously getting satisfaction from a child's behaviour, whilst she thinks she is blaming it. These themes, however, do not concern this book; nor does it treat in detail the child's relation to his father. The reason for this is that almost all the evidence concerns the child's relation to his mother, which is without doubt in ordinary circumstances by far his most important relationship during these years. It is she who feeds and cleans him, keeps him warm, and comforts him. It is to his mother that he turns when in distress. In the young child's eyes father plays second fiddle and his value increases only as the child becomes more able to stand alone. Nevertheless, as the illegitimate child knows, fathers have their uses even in infancy. Not only do they provide for their wives to enable them to devote themselves unrestrictedly to the care of the infant and toddler, but, by providing love and companionship, they support the mother emotionally and help her maintain that harmonious contented mood in the atmosphere of which her infant thrives. In what follows, therefore, while continual reference will be made to the mother–child relation, little will be said of the father–

child relation; his value as the economic and emotional support of the mother will be assumed.

Theories which place the origins of mental disturbances in these intimate domestic events have their origin in the work of Sigmund Freud and that of other members of the psychoanalytic school which he founded. Indeed, a very large proportion of the research work which will be referred to in this book was done by psychiatrists and psychologists with this special outlook and training. These theories stand, of course, in strong contrast to the theories which lay all their stress on constitutional and inherited factors, making heredity responsible for almost everything. Suffice it to say that the relative importance of nature and nurture remains still to be determined. In this connexion, it is useful to remember that recent work on the study of human beings and animals before birth has produced a steady accumulation of evidence that harmful changes in the environment before birth may cause faults of growth and development exactly like those which have in the past been thought to be due to heredity. This is a finding of great importance, which, as will be seen, is exactly paralleled in psychology. It is to be emphasized, however, that such findings in no way contradict theories of the bad influence of hereditary factors, except in so far as people hold that hereditary factors *alone* account for all differences in human behaviour. Indeed, there is reason to believe that hereditary factors also play a part and that the greatest scientific progress will be made when the interaction of the two can be studied.

A second far-reaching biological principle also stems from the study of development before birth, namely, the discovery that the harmful effects on an unborn young animal or child of intoxication, infection, and other damage vary not only with the nature of the injury and the structure and function of the tissue mainly attacked, but also with the maturity of that tissue.

A particularly interesting example, which owes its discovery to an Australian surgeon, is that of the harm which can be done to an unborn baby if its mother catches German measles. If she has this illness very early in her pregnancy – between the sixth and tenth weeks – there is serious danger that the German measles virus will damage the unborn baby, especially its eyes and ears, which are just beginning to be formed at that time, and thus cause blindness or deafness. If she has the illness either earlier or later there is no danger of harm. There is thus a special period when the organ is just being formed when it is particularly liable to damage.

There is also plenty of reason to think that in just the same way emotional experiences at certain very early and special stages of mental life may have very vital and long-lasting effects. This has been shown to be true of birds and dogs in a number of studies made by European biologists. The behaviour of fully-grown birds to other members of their kind, including of course their mates, is greatly influenced by the sort of individual who has tended them in their earliest youth. In fact, so sensitive are many birds to who looks after them immediately after they hatch that, if they are then 'mothered' by a human being, they become deeply attached to human beings instead of to other birds, and later fall in love with human beings!

Fortunately the higher animals are not quite so sensitive as are birds to who cares for them in earliest infancy. Even so, we know that the person whom a dog selects to be his master is decided during puppy days. This is particularly true, for instance, of chows. If one wants to be sure of the loyalty of a chow one must rear him oneself, on no account starting with him after he is four or five months old.

These examples are perhaps sufficient to introduce the reader to the basic notion that what occurs in the earliest months and years of life can have deep and long-lasting effects and to show that the theories put forward in this book, far from being in themselves improbable, are in strict agreement with what biological science has shown to be true of both bodily and mental growth.

But before embarking on our review of all the sad results which can follow to babies who are unmothered, a word of reassurance to mothers may be timely. Some of them reading of the terrible damage which may be done to a child's personality by deprivation may become anxious lest they themselves are failing to give their babies what they need. Here it is necessary to insist on the fact that the cases which are described are those of children who have been completely deprived and left emotionally lonely and untended. It is exactly the kind of care which a mother gives without thinking that *is* the care which they have lacked. All the cuddling and playing, the intimacies of suckling by which a child learns the comfort of his mother's body, the rituals of washing and dressing by which through her pride and tenderness towards his little limbs he learns the value of his own, all these have been lacking. His mother's love and pleasure in him are his spiritual nourishment. Here again the comparison with physical health brings home the truth. A mother provides the needed food substances in her own milk in exactly the right combination without having to make a chemical analysis and work to a formula. It is only when nature's gifts are lacking that science must study what they are in order to make the best shift it can to replace them.

The absolute need of infants and toddlers for the continuous care of their mothers will be borne in on all who read this book, and some will exclaim 'Can I then never leave my child?' Though far more knowledge is required before a proper answer can be given, some advice is perhaps possible. In the first place, we must recognize that leaving any child of under three years of age is a major operation only to be undertaken for good and sufficient reasons, and, when undertaken, to be planned with great care. On no account should a child be placed with people he doesn't know, and for this reason relatives and neighbours are likely to be chosen. It is useful to have a transitional period of a few days during which time the mother and the substitute mother together care for the child, both to give the child a chance to adapt to the new person and to give the mother-substitute a chance to learn the child's likes and dislikes. The mother-substitute should be aware that the child will grieve for his mother, especially at bedtime, and will also be more clinging and demanding of her attention than an ordinary child of the same age. Favourite toys, too, will assume a very special value. A child of over about eighteen months may get some comfort from postcards and token presents sent him by his mother and the reassurance that she will soon return. These are always worth arranging whether they seem to be understood or not. Finally, the substitute mother must not be distressed if, when the mother returns, the child discards her like an outworn garment without so much as a thank you.

The mother herself must, of course, be prepared for her child to be upset on her return. Though he *may* fulfil her hopes by greeting her warmly, she must not be surprised if he is cool and stand-offish for a few hours or a day or two, and she must remember that he may not even recognize her – something which is a terrible blow to a mother's pride. Moreover, after he has responded to her, there may still be difficulties because he may become extremely clinging and demanding and jealous. If these anxieties of his are treated sympathetically things will gradually return to the usual, but should they last they are bound to be a nuisance.

Naturally a mother will keep the time she is away from her child as short as possible, though in some cases the length of time lies outside her control. The holiday whilst granny looks after the baby, which so many mothers and fathers of young children pine for, is best kept to a week or ten days.

After a child has reached about three years, rather longer holidays from children can be taken safely, provided always that the child is in the care of someone he likes and trusts and that the anxieties which will inevitably be aroused in him are recognized and respected.

Looking after babies and young children is time-consuming and trying for a mother, but the more she learns about the nature of the creature she is caring for the easier and more satisfying she will find it, in the same way as the gardener works more easily if he understands the nature of the plants he grows. Given this understanding, the normal mother can afford to rely on the prompting of her instincts in the happy knowledge that the tenderness they prompt is what her baby wants. 'This little pig went to market' is a first text-book in child care.

CHAPTER 2

How we can Study the Harm Done

1. OBSERVATIONS OF BABIES AND YOUNG CHILDREN

EVIDENCE that the deprivation of mother-love in early childhood can have a far-reaching effect on the mental health and personality development of human beings comes from many sources. It falls into three main classes:

(*a*) Studies, by direct observation, of the mental health and development of children in institutions, hospitals, and foster-homes, here called direct studies.

(*b*) Studies which investigate the early histories of adolescents or adults who have developed psychological illnesses, here called retrospective studies.

(*c*) Studies which follow up groups of children who have suffered deprivation in their early years with a view to determining their state of mental health, here called follow-up studies.

The extent to which these studies, undertaken by people of many nations, varied training, and, as often as not, ignorant of each others' conclusions, confirm and support each other is impressive. What each individual piece of work lacks in thoroughness, scientific reliability, or precision is largely made good by the agreement of the whole. Nothing in scientific method carries more weight than this. Divergent voices are few.

The direct studies are the most numerous. They make it plain that, when deprived of maternal care, a child's development is almost always retarded – physically, intellectually, and socially – and that symptoms of physical and mental illness may appear. Such evidence is disquieting, but sceptics may question whether the check is permanent and whether the symptoms of illness may not easily be overcome. The retrospective and follow-up studies make it clear that such optimism is not always justified and that some children are gravely damaged for life. This is a sombre conclusion, which must now be regarded as established.

There are, however, important features of the situation about which little is known. For instance, it is by no means clear why some children are damaged and some not. It may be that hereditary factors play a part, but before falling back on this explanation it is important to review what is known of the effect of such influences as the child's age, and the length and, especially, the degree of his deprivation, each of which there is reason to think is vital.

The three classes of evidence will now be reviewed with special attention to these three points, the age at which a child loses his mother's care, the length of time for which he is deprived of it, and the completeness of his lack of mothering.

Direct observations of the ill-effects on young children of complete deprivation of maternal care have been made by a large number of child specialists and have shown that the child's development may be affected physically, intellectually, emotionally, and socially. All children under about seven years of age seem to be in danger of injury, and some of the effects are clearly discernible within the first few weeks of life.

A number of investigators have studied in great detail the effect of the want of mother-care amongst babies in institutions. Their results are too complicated to give in detail here, but they all show that from the age of a few weeks many babies show the bad effect of separation from their mother. This evidence from a number of reputable workers leaves no room for doubt that the development of the institution infant is below the normal from a very early age. Amongst some of the symptoms noticed we learn that the deprived baby may fail to smile at a human face or respond to a 'coo', may have a poor appetite or in spite of good nourishment fail to gain weight, may sleep badly, and show no initiative.

A very careful study of infants' babbling and crying showed that babies from birth to six months in an orphanage were always less vocal than those in families, the difference being clearly noticeable before two months of age. This backwardness in 'talking' is especially characteristic of the institution child of all ages. Tests (rather like those by which the intelligence of older children is rated) have been worked out for measuring young children. In this way groups of children living under different conditions can be compared in their development. Using such a test four groups of babies in America were studied. There were sixty-one children from town homes, not specially selected in any way, there were twenty-three children of professional parents, eleven from peasant homes, and sixty-nine babies of delinquent unmarried mothers. All of them when first they were tested were from one to four months of age.

At this stage the 'professional' group were best developed, after them came the 'unselected' town group, then the peasant children and then the illegitimate babies. After eight months they were tested again. In the meanwhile all but the 'unselected' town group had been with their own mothers; this unselected town group had been in an institution. The second testing showed similar development for their ages in all the groups which had been with their mothers (though the 'professionals' did not lead by quite so much, and the 'illegitimates' had to some extent caught up), but the institution children had lost terribly, and were of a standard far below the normal for their age.

It is true that these infants were living in conditions especially bad from the psychological point of view, as not only was there but one nurse to some seven children, but, for reasons of hygiene, the children were kept restricted to cots and cubicles in what amounted to solitary confinement. However, other studies make it plain that retardation may occur in conditions which are far from being as bad as these. Twenty-nine children aged from six months to two and a half years (mostly between nine and fifteen months), all of whom were waiting adoption, were studied. All had been cared for by foster-mothers; fifteen with no other young children, the remainder with up to three others in the same foster-home. Those receiving all the foster-mother's attention were on the average ahead in development, while those who had to share it with other babies were retarded. Here is another story of infants awaiting adoption. One hundred and twenty-two babies, eighty-three cared for in an institution and thirty-nine in foster-homes, all of whom had come into the society's care within their first two months of life, had been tested around six months of age. Those in the institution were in one large nursery, which had accommodation for seventeen babies and was staffed by a total of ten practical nurses, there being never fewer than two in attendance during the day. The results of the tests were slightly above average for the foster-home children and slightly below for the institutionalized.

There are several studies showing similar retardation in the second and later years, from Austria, Denmark, France, and the U.S.A. In one thorough study of thirty children, aged thirty-four to thirty-five months, half of whom had lived in an institution and the other half in foster-homes from four months of age, the development of the foster-home group was found to be average, whilst that of the institution children bordered on the mentally defective. Another investigator compared a group of 113 children, aged between one and four years, almost all of whom had spent their whole lives in one of some twelve different institutions, with a comparable group who lived at home and attended day nurseries. The mothers of these latter children were working and the homes often very unsatisfactory. Even so, the average development of the family children was normal, while that of the institution children was retarded. This difference is found consistently at each of three age-levels, namely, children in the second, third, and fourth years of life.

Though there can be no mistaking that these findings all point the same way, their value is frequently questioned on the grounds that many children in institutions are born of parents of poor stock, physically and mentally, and that heredity alone might well account for all the differences. Those who make this objection do not seem to be aware that in the majority of the studies described care has been taken by the investigators to ensure that other groups of children, brought up either in their own home or in foster-homes and of a similar social class and as nearly as possible of similar stock, were studied at the same time for purposes of comparison. The only certain method of ruling out the effects of heredity is by comparing identical twins. Though there are no human twin studies of the problem, one psychologist is doing experimental work on twin goat kids, one of whom is separated from its mother for a brief spell each day and the other not. Except for the daily experimental period of forty minutes, both kids live with and feed from their mother. During the experimental period the lights are periodically extinguished, which is known to create anxiety in goats, and this produces very different behaviour in the twins. The one which is with its mother is at ease and moves about freely; the isolated one is 'psychologically frozen' and remains cowed in one corner. In one of the first experiments the isolated kid discontinued suckling from its mother and, the experimenters being unaware of this and so unable to help, it died after a few days. This is ample demonstration of the adverse effects of maternal deprivation on the young of mammals, and disposes finally of the argument that all the observed effects are due to heredity.

Moreover, positive evidence that the cause of these troubles is maternal deprivation comes from innumerable sources. First, there are very clear findings that the longer the deprivation the lower falls the child's development. Secondly, there is experimental evidence that even if the child remains in the same institution, extra mothering from a substitute will diminish the ill-effects. Nearly twenty years ago two groups of two-year-olds living in the same institution were studied. One group was given very little tenderness, although adequately cared for in every other respect, while in the other a nurse was assigned to each child and there was no lack of tenderness and affection. At the end of half a year the first group was mentally and physically retarded in comparison with the second.

Finally, there is the evidence of spectacular changes in a child's condition following restoration to his mother. One child specialist remarks:

> The rapidity with which the symptoms of hospitalism begin to disappear when an afflicted baby is placed in a good home is amazing. The baby promptly becomes more animated and responsive; fever, if present in the hospital, disappears in twenty-four to seventy-two hours; there is a gain in weight and an improvement in the colour.

He cites as an example a boy who at four months of age, the latter two in hospital, weighed less than at birth and whose condition was critical.

> His appearance was that of a pale, wrinkled old man. His breathing was so weak and superficial that it seemed as though he might stop breathing at any moment. When seen twenty-four hours after he had been at home he was cooing and smiling. Though no change had been made in his diet he started to gain promptly and by the end of the first year his weight was well within the normal range. He appeared to be in every way a normal child.

The dramatic and tragic changes in behaviour and feeling which follow separation of a young child from his mother and the beneficent results of restoring him to her are in fact available for all to see, and it is astonishing that so little attention has been given to them hitherto. So painful, indeed, are the agonies which these children suffer on separation that it may well be that those who have their care shut their eyes in self-protection. Yet of their existence there can be no doubt, as distressingly similar pictures are given by many different investigators.

The description of the typical separated infant – listless, quiet, unhappy, and unresponsive to a smile or a coo – has already been quoted. The infant's condition in the age-range of six to twelve months has been the subject of systematic study. It is undoubtedly a form of depression having many of the hallmarks of the typical adult depressive patient of the mental hospital. The emotional tone is one of apprehension and sadness. The child withdraws himself from all that is around him, there is no attempt to contact a stranger and no brightening if this stranger contacts him. Activities are retarded and the child often sits or lies inert in a dazed stupor. Lack of sleep is common and lack of appetite universal. Weight is lost and the child easily catches infection. There is a sharp drop in general development.

In what conditions, it may be asked, does this develop? In general, it is characteristic of infants who have had a happy relationship with their mothers up till six or nine months and are then suddenly separated from them without an adequate substitute being provided. Of ninety-five children on whom a diagnosis was made, 20 per cent reacted to separation by severe depression, and another 27 per cent by mild depression, making nearly 50 per cent in all. Almost all those with a close and loving relation to their mothers suffered, which means that the depressive response to separation is a normal one at this age. The fact that a majority of those with unhappy relationships escaped indicates that their inner development was already damaged and their later capacity for love likely to be impaired. The illness respected neither sex nor race – boys and girls, white and coloured, all being affected. Although recovery is rapid if a child is restored to his mother, the possibility of wounds to the spirit which may later become active cannot be disregarded, while, if the condition is permitted to continue, recovery is greatly impeded. Some observers believe that after three months of deprivation there is a qualitative change, after which recovery is rarely, if ever, complete.

It has been noticed that disturbances of development may also follow separation at an even earlier age. These disturbances are much less dramatic than in older babies and were at first described as 'mild depressions', but further observation made this term seem wholly inappropriate, since it became evident that the condition was neither mild nor could it properly be classified as depression. Those disturbances to which infants of the age group three to six months are prone do not show themselves so quickly.

These very adverse results, it must be emphasized, can be partially avoided during the first year of life by the children being mothered by a substitute. Hitherto many have thought that substitute care could be completely successful during most of this year. Some observers, however, are now definitely of the opinion that damage is frequently done by changes even as early as three months. Nevertheless, all are agreed that substitute care, even if not wholly adequate, is indispensable and should always be given. In the second and third years of life, the emotional response to separation is not only just as severe, but substitute mothers are often rejected out of hand, a child becoming acutely and inconsolably distressed for a period of days, a week, or even more, without a break. During much of this time he is in a state of agitated despair and either screaming or moaning. Food and comfort are alike refused. Only exhaustion brings sleep. After some days he becomes quieter and may relapse into apathy, from which he slowly emerges to take more interest in his strange environment. For some weeks or even months, however, he may show a return to babyish behaviour. He wets his bed, masturbates, gives up talking, and insists on being carried, so that the less experienced nurse may suppose him to be mentally defective.

Naturally there are very many variations of reaction in

this age group and not all children respond in the way described; and once again it appears to be the children who have had the most intimate and happy relationship with their mothers who suffer most. Those who have been brought up in institutions and have had no permanent mother-figure show no responses of this kind at all, the result of their emotional life already having been damaged. Though an inexperienced nurse welcomes the child who regards one adult as being as good as another and criticizes the 'family baby', who reacts violently as having been 'spoilt', all the evidence suggests that a violent reaction is normal and an apathetic resignation a sign of unhealthy development.

Those who are reluctant to admit the reality and possible seriousness of these reactions often express the belief that a little wise management can easily avoid them. Though much further research is required, there is good reason for believing that the prevention of such responses is very difficult. It is common knowledge that children in their second and third years in hospital are acutely upset after being visited by their parents, and skilled efforts to avoid this happening do not meet with success. Moreover, Mrs Burlingham and Miss Anna Freud, who had several years' experience of these problems while running a residential nursery in Hampstead during the Second World War, and who made every effort to make the change from home to nursery easy for a child, were by no means always successful. In one of their monthly reports they write:

> In dealing with new cases of this kind we have attempted to work out a process of 'separation in slow stages' so as to mitigate its consequences for the child. Though this has proved beneficial with children from three or four years onward, we have found that *very little can be done to prevent regression* [i.e. return to more infantile behaviour] *where children between one and a half and two and a half are concerned*. Infants of that age can stand sudden changes and separations of a day's length without any visible effect. Whenever it is more than that they tend to lose their emotional ties, revert in their instincts and regress in their behaviour. [Authors' italics.]

They illustrate this difficulty by giving a full account of the behaviour of a boy of twenty-four months who was a well-developed easy child with a good relation to his mother. Despite being looked after by the same mother-substitute and being visited by his mother during the first week of his stay, his behaviour deteriorated when she reduced her visits to two a week, and when she gave up visiting he regressed severely.

He became listless, often sat in a corner sucking and dreaming, at other times he was very aggressive. He almost completely stopped talking. He was dirty and wet continually, so that we had to put nappies on him. He sat in front of his plate eating very little, without pleasure, and started smearing his food over the table. At this time the nurse who had been looking after him fell ill, and Bobby did not make friends with anyone else, but let himself be handled by everyone without opposition. A few days later he had tonsillitis and went to the sickroom. In the quiet atmosphere there he seemed not quite so unhappy, played quietly, but generally gave the impression of a baby. He hardly ever said a word, had entirely lost his bladder and bowel control, sucked a great deal. On his return to the nursery he looked very pale and tired. He was very unhappy after rejoining the group, always in trouble and in need of help and comfort. He did not seem to recognize the nurse who had looked after him at first.

The long-term after-effects on children of these harrowing experiences can sometimes be calamitous and are discussed later. The immediate after-effects, although not always evident to an untrained observer, are also frequently very disquieting to the expert. Those most commonly observed are (*a*) a hostile reaction to the mother on reunion with her, which sometimes takes the form of a refusal to recognize her; (*b*) an excessive demandingness towards the mother or substitute mother, in which intense possessiveness is combined with insisting on his own way, acute jealousy, and violent temper tantrums; (*c*) a cheerful but shallow attachment to any adult within the child's orbit; and (*d*) an apathetic withdrawal from all emotional entanglements, combined with monotonous rocking of the body and sometimes head banging. These reactions have been observed by many child specialists.

A special note of warning must be sounded regarding the children who respond apathetically or by a cheerful undiscriminating friendliness, since people ignorant of the principles of mental health are habitually deceived by them. Often they are quiet, obedient, easy to manage, well-mannered and orderly, and physically healthy; many of them even appear happy. So long as they remain in the institution there is no obvious ground for concern, yet when they leave they go to pieces, and it is evident that their adjustment had a hollow quality and was not based on a real growth of personality. Satisfaction is also expressed on occasion that a child has completely forgotten his mother. Not only is this usually not true, as he shows when he cries for her when in distress, but when it is true it is very serious, for it is on the steady growth and expansion of this relationship that his future mental health depends.

Naturally the particular kinds of reactions shown by different children will vary, and will depend greatly on the conditions in which they are living. The coming of a mother-substitute may change a group of apathetic or amiably undiscriminating children into possessive and tempestuous little savages. On the introduction of a substitute mother in the Hampstead nursery mentioned above:

Children, who have shown themselves adaptable and accommodating under group conditions, suddenly become insufferably demanding and unreasonable. Their jealousy and, above all, their possessiveness of the beloved grown-up may be boundless. It easily becomes compulsive where the mother-relationship is no new experience, but where separation from a real mother or (and) a former foster-mother has occurred before. The child is all the more clinging, the more it has an inner conviction that separation will repeat itself. Children become disturbed in their play activities when they watch anxiously whether their 'own' nurse leaves the room on an errand or for her off-hour or whether she has any intimate dealings with children outside her family. Tony, three and a half for instance, would not allow Sister Mary to use 'his' hand for handling other children. Jim, two to three, would burst into tears whenever his 'own' nurse left the room. Shirley, four years, would become intensely depressed and disturbed when 'her' Marion was absent for some reason, etc. It is true that all these children had had to cope with a series of traumatic [i.e. hurtful] separations in their lives.

Many a mother whose young child has been away from her a few weeks or months can confirm and enlarge upon such observations. Sometimes on reunion a child is emotionally frozen, unable to express his feelings, sometimes unable even to speak. Then, in a torrent, his feelings thaw. Tearful sobs are succeeded (in those able to speak) by an accusing 'Why did you leave me, Mummy?' Thenceforward for many weeks or months he never allows his mother out of his sight, he is babyish, anxious, and easily angered. Wisely handled, these troubles may gradually fade away, though once again the real possibility of unseen psychic scars must not be forgotten which may become active and give rise to emotional illness in later life. That this is a real danger is made clear by observation of sudden panics in children, who have apparently recovered emotional balance, when confronted by someone whom they associate with the separation experience. If the babyish anxious behaviour on return home is unsympathetically handled, vicious circles in the child's relation to his mother develop, bad behaviour being met by rebuffs and punishments, which in their turn call forth more babyishness, more demands, more tempers. In this way develops the unstable neurotic personality, unable to come to terms with himself or the world, unable especially to make loving and loyal relationships with other people.

Disturbing though such a sequence of events may be, it is almost certainly less sinister than the case of the child who responds either by withdrawing into himself or by undiscriminating and shallow friendliness. These responses, which are probably the result of frequent separations or of prolonged separation occurring before about two and a half years of age and without a substitute mother-person being available, are the forerunners of the grave personality disturbances (known technically as psychopathic) which are described fully in the next chapter.

At what age, it may be asked, does a child cease being liable to damage by a lack of maternal care? All who have studied the matter would agree that between three and five years the risk is still serious, though much less so than earlier. During this period children no longer live exclusively in the present, and can consequently conceive dimly of a time when their mothers will return, which is impossible to most children younger than three. Furthermore, the ability to talk permits of simple explanations, and the child will take more readily to understanding mother-substitutes. During this age-period, therefore, it may be said that wise and understanding management can go far to lessen ill-effects, though in its absence very serious reactions, comparable to those of the child between one and three, are not uncommon.

After the age of five the risk diminishes still further, though there can be no reasonable doubt that a fair proportion of children between the ages of five and seven or eight are unable to adjust satisfactorily to separations, especially if they are sudden and there has been no preparation. A vivid and distressing picture has been given by a now grown-up patient, of what it felt like for a boy of six to be confined to hospital for three years. He describes 'the desperate homesickness and misery of the early weeks [which] gave way to indifference and boredom during the subsequent months'. He describes how he made a passionate attachment to the matron which compensated for the loss of home, but how, on returning, he felt out of place and an intruder. 'In the end, this barrenness led me away from home again . . . but no second mother-figure came my way, and indeed I was not then capable of creating stable relationships . . . my responses were exaggerated, often uncalled for, and I became extremely moody and depressed . . . I also became aggressive.' Finally, after describing how he had, in later years, gained some understanding of himself, he writes: 'I still have aggressions. . . . They take the unfortunate form of making me excessively intolerant of my own faults in other people, and are therefore a menace to my relationship with my own children.' The difficulty for deprived children to become successful parents is perhaps the most damaging of all the effects of deprivation, a point emphasized later in this book.

Confirmation of this picture is given by a set of valuable case-histories of some dozens of children whose neurotic symptoms had either developed or been made worse by separation from the mother, most of the separation experiences being in hospital. In about half of them the experience of separation occurred during the first three years, in the other half between about three and eight years. In many of the latter the children could describe clearly how they had felt in hospital, common anxieties being the beliefs either that they would not return home, or that they were being sent away for being naughty. Thus a boy of seven and a half who had been three times in hospital or convalescent home since the age of three and a half remarked: 'I thought I was never coming home again because I was only six years old. I heard my sister say they were going to dump me and that I'd never come home again'. Another child, a girl of six and three-quarters, when being sent to fever hospital in her third year, had cried: 'I will be a good girl – don't send me'. On returning home, she was very quiet and sat scared in a corner much of the time. Though she never talked of this experience, she would play elaborate hospital games with her dolls in which sending them away to hospital was a punishment for naughtiness.

In the surveys of evacuated children between the ages of five and sixteen undertaken during the late war, there were a sufficient number of reports of an adverse response to confirm this account and to make it clear that children of this age are not yet emotionally self-supporting. Teachers reported that homesickness was prevalent and power of concentration in schoolwork declined. Bedwetting, nervous symptoms, and delinquency increased. Though in many cases these responses passed off and had no serious after-effects, in others the problems persisted on return home.

While there is reason to believe that all children under three, and a great many between three and five, suffer through deprivation, in the case of those between five and eight it is probably only a minority, and the question arises – why some and not others? Contrary to what we find in the younger age-groups, for children of this age the better their relation to their mothers the better they can tolerate separation. A happy child, secure in his mother's love, is not made unbearably anxious; the insecure child, doubtful of his mother's good feelings towards him, may easily misinterpret events. These misinterpretations, moreover, may smoulder on unknown to anyone, almost unknown to the child himself. The belief that he has been sent away for naughtiness leads to anxiety and hatred, and these in turn to a vicious circle in his relations to his parents. Thus children aged five or eight, who are already liable to emotional troubles, can easily be made far worse by a separation experience, whereas secure children of the same age may come through almost unscathed. Even so, for both groups much will depend on how the child is prepared for the situation, how he is treated during it, and how his mother handles him on his return.

CHAPTER 3

How we can Study the Harm Done

II. OBSERVATIONS OF OLDER CHILDREN WHO WERE DEPRIVED IN INFANCY

SOME of the immediately bad effects of deprivation on young children and some of the short-term after-effects have now been discussed, and note taken that those without training in mental health are apt either to deny the existence of such responses or to waive them aside as of no consequence. In this chapter, the tremendous weight of evidence will be reviewed which makes it clear that those who view these responses with concern, so far from crying wolf, are calling attention to matters of grave medical and social significance.

During the late 1930s, at least six independent workers were struck by the frequency with which children who committed numerous delinquencies, who seemed to have no feelings for anyone and were very difficult to treat, were found to have had grossly disturbed relationships with their mothers in their early years. Persistent stealing, violence, egotism, and sexual misdemeanours were among their less pleasant characteristics.

One of the first cases recorded still stands as typical:

My first example is an eight-year-old girl who was adopted a year and a half before being examined. After an illegitimate birth, the child was shifted about from one relative to another, finally brought to a child-placing agency, and then placed in a foster-home for two months before she came to the adoptive parents. The complaints were lying and stealing. The parents described the child's reaction to the adoption as very casual. When they took her home and showed her the room she was to have all for herself, and took her on a tour of the house and grounds, she showed apparently no emotional response. Yet she appeared very vivacious and 'affectionate on the surface'. After a few weeks of experience with her, the adoptive mother complained to her husband that the child did not seem able to show any affection. The child, to use the mother's words, 'would kiss you but it would mean nothing'. The husband told his wife that she was expecting too much, that she should give the child a chance to get adapted to the situation. The mother was somewhat mollified by these remarks, but still insisted that something was wrong. The father said he saw nothing wrong with the child. In a few months, however, he made the same complaint. By this time, also, it was noted that the child was deceitful and evasive. All methods of correction were of no avail. . . . The schoolteacher complained of her general inattention and her lack of pride in the way her things looked. However, she did well in her school subjects, in keeping with her good intelligence. She also made friends with children, though none of these were close friendships. After a contact of a year and a half with the patient the adoptive father said, 'You just can't get to her', and the mother remarked, 'I have no more idea today what's going on in that child's mind than I knew the day she came. You can't get under her skin. She never tells what she's thinking or what she feels. She chatters but it's all surface.'

Here, in brief, are many of the typical features:

superficial relationships;
no real feeling – no capacity to care for people or to make true friends;
an inaccessibility, exasperating to those trying to help;
no emotional response to situations where it is normal – a curious lack of concern;
deceit and evasion, often pointless;
stealing;
lack of concentration at school.

The only item in this case which is not typical is the child's good schoolwork, as more often than not this is seriously interfered with.

Between 1937 and 1943 there were many papers on this subject, several of which originated independently and some of which were completed in ignorance of the work of others.

The unanimity of their conclusions stamps their findings as true. With monotonous regularity each observer put his finger on the child's inability to make relationships as being the central feature from which all the other disturbances sprang, and on the history of long periods spent in an institution or, as in the case quoted, of the child's being shifted about from one foster-mother to another as being its cause. So similar are the observations and the conclusions – even the very words – that each might have written the others' papers:

> The symptom complaints are of various types. They include, frequently, aggressive and sexual behaviour in early life, stealing, lying, often of the fantastic type, and, essentially, complaints variously expressed that indicate some lack of emotional response in the child. It is this lack of emotional response, this shallowness of feeling that explains the difficulty in modifying behaviour.

> Early in the work a third group of girls was recognized who were asocial [i.e. unaware of obligations to others], but not obviously neurotic, and with whom no treatment methods seemed of any avail. Later it became clear that the feature common to them was an inability to make a real relationship with any member of the staff. There might seem to be a good contact, but it invariably proved to be superficial. . . . There might be protestations of interest and a boisterous show of affection, but there was littie or no evidence of any real attachment having been made. In going over their previous history, this same feature was outstanding. . . . [These girls] have apparently had no opportunity to have a loving relationship in early childhood [and] seem to have little or no capacity to enter into an emotional relation with another person or with a group.

> All the children [twenty-eight in number] present certain common symptoms of inadequate personality development chiefly related to an inability to give or receive affection; in other words, inability to relate the self to others. . . . The conclusion seems inescapable that infants reared in institutions undergo an isolation type of experience, with a resulting isolation type of personality.

Two special problems were referred to the ward from two child-placing agencies. One came from an agency [in which] there is a feeling that no attachment should be allowed to develop between the child and the boarding home, so that by the time the child is five years old, he has no attachment to anybody and no pattern of behaviour. . . . Another special group consisted of children placed in infancy [who] are given the best pediatric care . . . but have been deprived of social contacts and play materials. . . . These children are unable to accept love, because of their severe deprivation in the first three years. . . . They have no play pattern, cannot enter into group play and abuse other children. . . . They are overactive and distractible; they are completely confused about human relationships. . . . This type of child does not respond to the nursery group and continues overactive, aggressive and asocial.

'Imperviousness and a limited capacity for affective relationships' characterize children who have spent their early years in an institution, 'Can it be that the absence of affective relationship in infancy made it difficult or even unnecessary for the institution children to participate later in positive emotional relationships . . . ?'

These communications came from across the Atlantic: meanwhile quite independent observations by Dr Bowlby in London led to exactly the same conclusions:

Prolonged breaks [in the mother–child relationship] during the first three years of life leave a characteristic impression on the child's personality. Such children appear emotionally withdrawn and isolated. They fail to develop loving ties with other children or with adults and consequently have no friendships worth the name. It is true that they are sometimes sociable in a superficial sense, but if this is scrutinized we find that there are no feelings, no roots in these relationships. This, I think, more than anything else, is the cause of their hard-boiledness. Parents and school-teachers complain that nothing you say or do has any effect on the child. If you thrash him he cries for a bit, but there is no emotional response to being out of favour, such as is normal to the ordinary child. It appears to be of no essential consequence to these lost souls whether they are in favour or not. Since they are unable to make genuine emotional relations, the condition of relationship at a given moment lacks all significance for them. . . . During the last few years I have seen some sixteen cases of this affectionless type of persistent pilferer and in only two was a prolonged break absent. In all the others gross breaches of the mother–child relation had occurred during the first three years, and the child had become a persistent pilferer.

Since these early papers there have been several careful 'retrospective studies', namely, studies made by specialists who were called upon to treat nervous symptoms and disturbances of behaviour, who by working back into the children's histories, unearthed the common factors of lack of care – caused either by their being in institutions, or being posted, like parcels, from one mother-figure to another.

One doctor in a large New York hospital had some 5,000 children under her care from 1935 to 1944. She found that from 5 per cent to 10 per cent of them showed the characteristics which have already been described.

There is an inability to love or feel guilty. There is no conscience. Their inability to enter into any relationship makes treatment or even education impossible. They have no idea of time, so that they cannot recall past experience and cannot benefit from past experience or be motivated to future goals. This lack of time concept is a striking feature in the defective organization of the personality structure. . . .

Ten of the children referred to were seen five years later. They 'all remained infantile, unhappy, and affectionless and unable to adjust to children in the schoolroom or other group situation'.

Dr Bowlby, writing of the children he dealt with in London, described how in some of their histories it was possible to find how the child had reacted to some startling and painful happening. He laid especial emphasis on the tendency of these children to steal. Dividing all the cases he had seen at a child guidance clinic into those who had been reported as stealing and those who had not, he compared a group of forty-four thieves with a control group, similar in number, age, and sex, who although emotionally disturbed did not steal. The thieves were distinguished from the controls in two main ways. First, there were among them fourteen 'affectionless characters', while there were none in the control group. Secondly, seventeen of the thieves had suffered complete and prolonged separation (six months or more) from their mothers or established foster-mothers during their first five years of life; only two of the controls had suffered similar separations. Neither of these differences can be accounted for by chance. Two further points of great importance were that the 'affectionless characters' almost always had a history of separation, and that they were far more delinquent than any of the others.

The results showed that bad heredity was less frequent amongst the 'affectionless' thieves than amongst the others: of the fourteen children who came into this class only three could be said to have had a bad heredity (i.e. parents or grandparents with serious psychological ill-health), but twelve of them had histories of separation from their mothers. Thus there can be no doubting that for the affectionless thief nurture not nature is to blame.

Dr. Bowlby concludes:

> There is a very strong case indeed for believing that prolonged separation of a child from his mother (or mother substitute) during the first five years of life stands foremost among the causes of delinquent character development.*

Among the cases described is one of a boy who was believed to have had a good relation to his mother until the age of eighteen months, but who was then in hospital for nine months, during which time visiting by his parents was forbidden. Other cases suggest that hospitalization and changes of mother-figure as late as the fourth year can have

* This statement has often been challenged. Recent evidence is discussed on page 229.

very destructive effects in producing the development of an affectionless psychopathic character given to persistent delinquent conduct and extremely difficult to treat.

Other retrospective studies touch on this problem. Thus the record of some 200 children under the age of twelve seen at a child-guidance clinic in London during the years 1942–6, whose troubles seemed to have been caused or aggravated by the war, showed that in one-third of the cases the trouble had been caused by evacuation. Almost all the difficult and long treatment cases were due to evacuation, not, it must be emphasized, to experience of bombing. No less than two-thirds of the children who presented problems after evacuation had been under the age of five when first evacuated. Since the number of young children evacuated in proportion to older ones was small, the figures make clear the extent to which it is especially the young child who is damaged by experiences of this kind.

Again, studies of adult patients have often led their authors to the conclusion that love deprivation is the cause of their psychological condition. Writing of hysterical patients, one doctor puts forward the view that

> regardless of the nature of the individual's inborn tendencies, he will not develop hysteria unless he is subjected during childhood to situations causing him to crave affection.

Among such situations he lists the death of a parent and separation of child from parents. Another doctor who collected information on 530 prostitutes in Copenhagen, found that one-third of them had not been brought up at home, but had spent their childhood under troubled and shifting conditions.

> Three per cent were brought up by close relations, 3 per cent were boarded out or sent to a home, 27 per cent were raised under combined conditions, partly in homes or almshouses, partly in institutions for the feeble-minded or epileptics, partly at home or with relatives.

Sometimes they had had three or four different foster-homes during the course of their childhood. Seventeen per cent of the total were illegitimate.

The objection to all these retrospective studies is, of course, that they are concerned only with children who have developed badly and fail to take into account those who may have had the same experience, but have developed normally. We now come to studies of special value, since they take a group of children placed as infants in institutions and seek to discover how they have turned out.

One very careful investigation carried out by a New York psychologist, Dr Goldfarb, was scientifically planned from the beginning to test the theory that the experience of living in the highly impersonal surroundings of an institution nursery in the first two or three years of life has an adverse effect on personality development. What he did was to compare the mental development of children, brought up until the age of about three in an institution and then placed in foster-homes, with others who had gone straight from their mothers to foster-homes, in which they had remained. In both groups the children had been handed over by their mothers in infancy, usually within the first nine months of life. Dr Goldfarb took great care to see that the two groups were of similar heredity. The children most thoroughly studied consisted of fifteen pairs who, at the time of the examination, ranged in age from ten to fourteen years. One set of fifteen was in the institution from about six months of age to three and a half years, the other set had not had this experience. Conditions in the institution were of the highest standards of physical hygiene, but lacked the elementary essentials of mental hygiene:

> Babies below the age of nine months were each kept in their own little cubicles to prevent the spread of epidemic infection. Their only contacts with adults occurred during these few hurried moments when they were dressed, changed, or fed by nurses.

Later they were members of a group of fifteen or twenty under the supervision of one nurse, who had neither the training nor the time to offer them love or attention. As a result they lived in 'almost complete social isolation during the first year of life', and their experience in the succeeding two years was only slightly richer. Dr Goldfarb has gone to great pains to ensure that the foster-homes of the two groups are similar, and shows further that, in respect of the mother's occupational, educational, and mental standing, the institution group was slightly superior to the controls. Any differences in the mental states of the two groups of children are, therefore, almost certain to be the result of their differing experiences in infancy. We must remember that none of the children had had the advantage of a quite unbroken home life. All had been in their foster-homes for six or seven years. Yet the differences between the groups are very marked and painfully full of meaning.

The two groups of children were studied by a great variety of tests. In intelligence, in power of abstract thinking, in their social maturity, their power of keeping rules or making friends, the institution group fell far below those who had stayed with their mothers for some months and then gone straight to the care of foster-mothers. Only three of the fifteen institution children were up to the average in speech, whilst all fifteen of the others reached this level. This continuing backwardness of speech has been noticed by many other observers – it looks as though the art of speech must be learnt at the right time and in the right place.

Whilst it will be seen that in most respects Dr Goldfarb's conclusions are much like those of other observers, it must be noted that in two respects they differ from Dr Bowlby's. First, the New York children 'craved affection' and the London ones are observed to be 'affectionless'. This contrast is probably more apparent than real. Many 'affectionless' characters crave affection, but none the less have an almost complete inability either to accept or reciprocate it. The poor capacity of all but two of Goldfarb's children for making relationships clearly confirms other work. The fact that only one of this group of Goldfarb's institution children stole and none truanted is, however, surprising in view of Bowlby's findings. The difference is probably valid and needs explanation: perhaps it can be explained this way. All of Goldfarb's cases had been institutionalized from soon after birth until they were three years old. None of Bowlby's had – they were all products of deprivation for a limited period, or of frequent changes. It may well be that their stealing was an attempt to secure love and gratification and so reinstate the love relationship which they had lost, whereas Goldfarb's cases, never having experienced anything of the kind, had nothing to reinstate. Certainly it would appear that the more complete the deprivation is in the early years the more indifferent to society and isolated a child becomes, whereas the more his deprivation is broken by moments of satisfaction the more he turns against society and suffers from conflicting feelings of love and hatred for the same people.

Before we leave the subject of Dr Goldfarb's writings, we must make it clear that we must not take it for granted that all infants and toddlers in institutions have similar experiences. Not only is it clear that they do not, but the more one studies all the evidence on the subject the more one becomes convinced that the outcome is to a high degree dependent on the exact nature of the psychological experience. If further research is to be fruitful, it must pay minute attention not only to the ages and periods of deprivation, but also to the quality of a child's relation to his mother before deprivation, his experiences with mother-substitutes, if any, during separation, and the reception he gets from his mother or foster-mother when at last he becomes settled again.

There are several other follow-up studies which, though far less thorough, show similar results. An American psychiatrist, Dr Lowrey, studied a group of children comprising among others twenty-two unselected cases who, with one exception, had been admitted to an institution before their first birthday and had remained there until they were three or four, when they were transferred to another society for fostering. They were examined when they were five years of age or older. All of them showed severe personality disturbances centring on an inability to give or receive affection. Symptoms, each of which occurred in half or more of them, included aggressiveness, negativism (contrariness or obstinacy), selfishness, excessive crying, food difficulties, speech defects, and bedwetting. Other difficulties only a little less frequent included over-activity, fears, and soiling.

Both Dr Goldfarb and Dr Lowrey report 100 per cent of children institutionalized in their early years to have developed very poorly; other studies show that many such children achieve a tolerable degree of social adaptation when adult. Though this finding is in accordance with the expectations of the man in the street, it would be a mistake to build too much on it, since it is known that very many people who are psychologically disturbed are able to make an apparent adjustment for long periods. Moreover, these other studies show a large proportion of obvious mental ill-health which the authors regard as confirming the harmfulness of institutional conditions for young children.

As long ago as 1924, a comprehensive study was made in the U.S.A. of the social adjustment as adults of 910 people who had been placed in foster-homes as children. A particularly interesting comparison is made between ninety-five of them who had spent five years or more of their childhood in institutions and eighty-four who had spent the same years at home (in 80 per cent of cases in bad homes). Not only had all the children of both groups, later, been placed in foster-homes of similar quality and at similar ages, but so far as could be determined the heredity of the two groups was similar. The results show that those brought up in an institution adjusted significantly less well than those who had remained during their first five years in their own homes. Since the two groups were probably of similar heredity, the difference cannot be explained in this way. The fact that no less than one-third of the institution children turned out to be 'socially incapable', of which nearly half were troublesome and delinquent, is to be noted.

It will be remarked, however, that, despite the institutional experience in the early years, two-thirds turned out 'socially capable'. So far as it goes this is satisfactory, but, as no expert examination was carried out, psychological troubles not leading to social incompetence were not recorded.

So far all the evidence has pointed in but one direction. It is now time to consider three studies which present evidence which calls these conclusions in question. It may be said at once that none of them is of high scientific quality. One is a brief note, questioning the accuracy of Dr Lowrey's 100 per cent bad results in some institutions, by another specialist who states that he has seen some sixteen children coming from the same institution and having had the same experiences as Lowrey's group, and that only two showed adverse features of personality. No details are given and there appears to have been no systematic investigation of the individual cases.

Another critic compares a group of 100 boys aged nine to fourteen years living in an institution with another 100 of the same age living at home in bad surroundings, where broken homes and family discords predominate. Using questionnaires, he shows that the two groups are similar in mental ill-health. Not only is a questionnaire an unsatisfactory way of measuring mental health, but no evidence is given regarding the age at which the children entered the institution.

The most recent of the three studies was carried out by a group of child-guidance workers in England. They compared the 'social maturity' of two groups of fifteen-year-old children: fifty-one who had spent the previous three years or more in an institution, and a comparable fifty-two who had lived at home. They showed that, although the institution children have a lower score than the family children, when the cases are regrouped according to their heredity an exactly similar difference is to be seen. On the basis of these figures they conclude that the case of those who argue that any social or personal retardation is attributable exclusively or mainly to environmental influences is weakened, and that constitutional factors are at least as important as environmental factors in the growth of social maturity.

These conclusions are ill-judged and certainly cannot be sustained by the evidence presented. In addition to technical criticism of the methods used in the inquiry, it is pointed out that some of the institution children did not enter until they were quite old, the average age of admission being four years; while, even more serious, of the family children in the control group, no less than twenty-two had been evacuated from their homes during the war, the average length of time being one year and nine months. Work with so many shortcomings cannot be accepted as calling in question the almost unanimous findings of the workers already quoted.

There is one other group of facts which is sometimes quoted as casting doubt on these findings – that from the Jewish communal settlements in Israel known as *kibbutz* (plural, *kibbutzim*). In these settlements, largely for ideological reasons, children are brought up by professional nurses in a 'Children's House'. Babies are reared in groups of five or six, and are later merged at the age of three years into larger groups numbering twelve to eighteen. The emphasis is throughout on communal rather than family care. Is not this, it may be asked, a clear example that communal care can be made to work without damaging the children? Before answering this question it is necessary to look more carefully at the conditions in which the children are raised. The following account is taken partly from the report of an American psychiatric social worker who recently visited Israel, and partly from a personal communication from the

Lasker Child Guidance Centre in Jerusalem. Both describe life in certain of the non-religious Kibbutzim. The former remarks:

> Separation is a relative concept and separation as it appears in the Kibbutz should not be thought of as identical with that of children who are brought up in foster-homes or institutions away from their parents. ... In the Kibbutz there is a great deal of opportunity for close relationship between child and parents.

Not only does the mother nurse her baby and feed him in the early months, but, to follow the Lasker Centre's description:

> once the suckling tie between mother and child is abandoned, the daily visit of the child to the room of the parents becomes the focus of family life for the child, and its importance is scrupulously respected. During these few hours the parents, or at least one of them, are more or less completely at the disposal of the children; they play with them, talk to them, carry the babies about, take the toddlers for little walks, etc.

The time spent with the children 'may amount to as much as two to three hours on working days and many more on the Sabbath'.

Here, then, is no complete abandonment of parent–child relations. Though the amount of time parents spend with their young children is far less than in most other Western communities, the report makes it clear that 'the parents are extremely important people in the children's eyes, and the children in the parents'. It is interesting to note, too, that the trend is steadily towards parents taking more responsibility. Formerly parents had to visit the children in the Children's House – now the children come to the parents' room and the parents even prepare light meals for them; feasts are now celebrated in the parents' room as well as communally in the Children's House; mothers are asserting themselves and demanding to see more of their children.

Finally, it is by no means certain that the children do not suffer from this regime. While both observers report good and cooperative development in adolescence, the Lasker Centre think there are signs of a somewhat higher level of insecurity among Kibbutz children than among others, at least until the age of seven years. They also point out that the strong morale and intimate group life of the Kibbutz are of great value to the older child and adolescent, and that these may offset some of the unsettlement of earlier years.

From this brief account it is evident that there is no evidence here which can be held to undermine our conclusions. The conditions provide, of course, unusually rich opportunities for research in child development, and it is to be hoped that these will not be missed.

Observations of War Orphans and Refugees

Evidence of the adverse effects on children of all ages of separation from their families was provided on a tragic scale during the Second World War, when thousands of refugee children from occupied lands in Europe were cared for in Switzerland and elsewhere. Owing to the scale of the problem, there was little time for systematic research, and in any case the children had been submitted to such diverse and often horrifying experiences that it would have been almost impossible to have isolated the effects of separation from those of other experiences. A summary of the findings of medical, educational, and relief workers emphasizes that 'while the reports tell of disturbances in character resulting from war, they show also the fundamental part played in their causation by rupture of the family tie'. Of experiences with refugee children at the Pestalozzi Village at Trogen, Switzerland, we read:

> No doubt remains that a long period without individual attention and personal relationships leads to mental atrophy; it slows down or arrests the development of the emotional life and thus in turn inhibits normal intellectual development. We have observed that acute psychical traumata [damaging experiences], however serious, do not result in such deep injury as chronic deficiencies and prolonged spiritual solitude.

In 1944 a small comparative study was made of ninety-seven Jewish refugee children in homes in Switzerland and 173 Swiss children of about the same age (eleven to seventeen years). All the children were asked to write an essay on 'What I think, what I wish, and what I hope'. From a scrutiny of these essays it appeared that for the refugees separation from their parents was evidently their most tragic experience. In contrast, few of the Swiss children mentioned their parents, who were evidently felt to be a natural and inevitable part of life. Another great contrast was the refugee children's preoccupation with their suffering past, or with frenzied and grandiose ideas regarding the future. The Swiss children lived happily in the present, which for the refugee was either a vacuum or at best an unsatisfying transition. Deprived of all the things which had given life meaning, especially family and friends, they were possessed by a feeling of emptiness.

Another psychologist also studied refugee children in Switzerland and others in a concentration camp. He describes such symptoms as bedwetting and stealing, an inability to make relations and a consequent loss of ability to form ideals, an increase of aggression, and intolerance of frustration.

In the Netherlands after the war, a group of psychiatrists studied some thousands of children whose parents had been deported in 1942 and 1943 and who had been cared for in foster-homes, often from earliest infancy. They report that frequent changes of foster-home almost always had very adverse effects, leading a child to become withdrawn and apathetic. This was sometimes accompanied by a superficial sociability and, later, promiscuous sex-relationships. Some young children managed to weather a single change, but others could not stand even this, and developed symptoms such as anxiety, depression, excessive clinging, and bedwetting. Many of the children were still emotionally disturbed when examined after the war and in need of treatment. It was noted that those who had had good family relationships before separation could usually be helped to an adjustment, but that for those with a bad family background the outlook was poor.

Finally may be noted an extensive psychological and statistical study undertaken in Spain following the civil war on over 14,000 cases of neglected and delinquent children housed in the environs of Barcelona. Once again there is confirmation of the decisive and adverse role in character development played by the break-up of the family and the vital importance of family life for satisfactory social and moral development. Particularly interesting is the confirmation of Dr Goldfarb's findings regarding impaired mental development. The intelligence levels of the neglected and delinquent children are much below those of a control group. Lessened capacity for abstract thought is also noted – the evidence, in the investigator's opinion, pointing to the existence of a strong link between the development of the abstract mental faculties and the family and social life of the child. He notes especially the following characteristics of the neglected and delinquent child:

> Feeble and difficult attention due to his great instability. Very slight sense of objective realities, overflowing imagination and absolute lack of critical ability. Incapacity for strict abstraction and logical reasoning. Noteworthy backwardness in the development of language. . . .

The similarity of these observations on war orphans and refugees to those on other deprived children will not fail to impress the reader.

CHAPTER 4

What Observation has Shown

THE evidence has been reviewed at some length because until recent years people have discussed as though it were an open question whether deprivation causes psychiatric disturbances. We suggest that the evidence is now such that it leaves no room for doubt regarding the general proposition – that the prolonged deprivation of a young child of maternal care may have grave and far-reaching effects on his character and so on the whole of his future life. It is a proposition exactly similar in form to those regarding the evil after-effects of German measles before birth or deprivation of vitamin D in infancy.

Nevertheless, although the main proposition may be regarded as proven, knowledge of details remains deplorably small. It is as though it had been proved that an absence of vitamin D causes rickets and that calcium is in some way involved, but as yet nothing were known about the amounts required or the connexion between the two substances. That deprivation can have bad consequences is known, but how much deprivation children of different ages can withstand has not yet been determined. The evidence available may now be summarized and such conclusions drawn as are permissible.

In the first place, there is abundant evidence that deprivation can have adverse effects on the development of children (*a*) during the period of separation; (*b*) during the period immediately after restoration to maternal care; and (*c*) in at least a small proportion of cases permanently. The fact that some children seem to escape is of no consequence. The same is true if children drink tubercle-infected milk or are exposed to the virus of infantile paralysis. In both these cases a sufficient proportion of children is so severely damaged for no one to dream of intentionally exposing a child to such hazards. Deprivation of maternal care in early childhood is a danger of the same class.

Most of the evidence in respect of long-term effects refers to certain very grave disturbances following severe deprivation; it is easiest to work from these established connexions to those which are less well understood. The evidence suggests that three somewhat different experiences can each produce the 'affectionless' and delinquent character in some children:

(*a*) Lack of any opportunity for forming an attachment to a mother-figure during the first three years.

(*b*) Deprivation for a limited period – at least three months and probably more than six – during the first three or four years.

(*c*) Changes from one mother-figure to another during the same period.

Though the general results of these different experiences appear the same, it seems probable that closer study will reveal differences.

Though it may be true, as some workers believe, that children placed in institutions for short periods after the age of about two do not develop affectionless and isolated characters, we know of enough cases where children who have been handed on from one mother-figure to another during the third and fourth years have developed very anti-social characters and have been unable to make satisfactory relations with other people to make it clear that very evil results may follow even at this age. Naturally, the effects on personality development at any given age will depend on the exact nature of the experience to which the child is submitted, information about which is all too frequently missing from records. Indeed, one of the great shortcomings of present evidence is a lack of detail and precision on this point.

Though all workers on the subject are now agreed that

the first year of life is of vital importance, there is at present some debate regarding the age at which deprivation has the most evil consequences. Dr Bowlby, after reviewing his cases, noted that the separations which appeared to do harm had all occurred after the age of six months and in a majority after that of twelve months, from which he was inclined to conclude that separations and deprivations in the first six months of life were less important for the child's welfare than later ones. This has also been the view of Miss Anna Freud. It has, however, been called in question by others who attach especial importance to the first half year. Whatever the outcome of this debate, the study of Dr Goldfarb, in which he examines the social adjustment of adolescents in relation to the age at which they were admitted to the institution, points unmistakably to the special danger in which the child stands during the first year in comparison with later ones. Other American references to children in whom the deprivation was limited to the first year, and who none the less showed retardation and personality distortion, provide further evidence regarding the first year as a whole, though they do not contribute to the debate regarding the baby's sensitiveness during the first half of it in particular.

For the present, therefore, it may be recorded that deprivation occurring in the second half of the first year of life is agreed by all students of the subject to be of great significance and that many believe this to be true also of deprivation occurring in the first half, especially from three to six months. The balance of opinion, indeed, is that considerable damage to mental health can be done by deprivation in these months, a view which is unquestionably supported by the direct observations, already described, of the immediately harmful effects of deprivation on babies of this age.

There is, however, a further point – the time limit within which the provision of mothering can make good some at least of the damage done by deprivation in these early months. The comparative success of many babies adopted between six and nine months who have spent their first half-year in conditions of deprivation makes it virtually certain that, for many babies at least, provided they receive good mothering in time, the effects of early damage can be greatly reduced. What Dr Goldfarb's work demonstrates without any doubt is that such mothering is almost useless if delayed until after the age of two and a half years. In actual fact this upper age limit for most babies is probably before twelve months. But the probable existence of a safety limit should not give rise to complacency: the fact that it may be possible to make good some of the damage done by deprivation in the early months is no excuse for permitting it to be inflicted in the first place.

So much for the fully fledged forms of personality disorder and the experiences which produce them, now widely recognized by child psychiatrists. However, those concerned with this problem point to the existence of less startling conditions to which less severe deprivation can give rise and which are far and away more frequent. Not only are there many other forms of maladjusted personality, including hysterics, but many conditions of anxiety and depression almost certainly stem from deprivation experiences or have been made worse by them.

Such examples are seen in those adults whose social life represents a series of relationships with older people, every one of whom is a substitute mother. They may be single, or in combination, the point being simply that the patient must, throughout life, be in contact with a person from whom the same demands are made that were thwarted in the original experience with the mother. The life pattern then becomes dependent on maintaining such relationships. When one of them is broken there is a period of depression, or a feeling that 'something is terrifically lacking', until another relationship is made. Another type of reaction is seen in the form chiefly of excessive demands made on the person who is selected to satisfy the privations of early life. . . . The problem is always the same – excessive demands for food, for money, for privileges.

Not infrequently people with these troubles deny their existence by an excessive show of cheerfulness and activity. This is an attempt to convince themselves that God's in his heaven, all's right with the world, a state of affairs of which they are far from sure. Naturally this method meets with some success but, based as it is on a denial, is in constant danger of cracking and leaving its owner in a state of despair. Moreover, even while it succeeds, the press of activity and intolerance of frustration are very trying to others, while it not infrequently leads to delinquency.

Though such cases are sadly numerous, they are mercifully more open to treatment than the severe forms. On the immense task set by the treatment of the 'affectionless' and delinquent character all psychiatrists are agreed. Because of their almost complete inability to make relationships, the psychiatrist is robbed of his principal tool: he should, of course, be skilled in the management of patients who hate him; he has yet to learn methods of affecting for the better patients who have only the shallowest of feelings for him. For instance, psychological treatment was given over a period of some six years to eighty girls in a small home for delinquent girls between the ages of twelve and sixteen. Half were successes and half failures. Response to treatment was related neither to intelligence nor to heredity. Its relationship to the girls' early family experiences, however, was striking.

The failure in treatment of all those who had suffered rejection or had never had a loving relationship recalls Dr Goldfarb's remark that he has never seen 'even one example of significantly favourable response to treatment by traditional methods of child psychiatry'. Another doctor goes so far as to say that 'once the defect is created it cannot be corrected', and recommends that methods of care should make no attempt to cure or correct, but 'should be protective and should aim to foster a dependent relationship'. Others are more hopeful and believe that if the child is permitted to go back to completely babyish behaviour there is a chance of his developing afresh along better lines. The work done at the Children's Village at Skå, near Stockholm, is an example of a European experiment along these lines. There the children are encouraged to become highly dependent on their house-mother and are permitted to go back to such infantile behaviour as taking their food from a baby's feeding bottle. This, and similar experiments in the U.S.A., are conceived on sensible lines, though there is debate regarding the amount of control which should be exercised over the children. It will be many years before the success of these methods can be judged.

The evidence available suggests that nothing but prolonged residence with an adult, with insight into the problem, skill in handling it, and unlimited time to devote to her charge, is likely to be of much avail. This is not only very expensive, but could never be made available to more than a tiny fraction of cases. Far more practicable, and in the long run far cheaper, is to arrange methods of care for infants and toddlers which will prevent these conditions developing.

CHAPTER 5

Theoretical Problems

JUST how we develop as personalities and how this development depends on our being in constant touch with some one person who cares for us during the critical time in our early years, whilst our ability to adjust ourselves to the outside world of things and of people is growing, is a very interesting question. The problems raised are complicated, and as yet by no means clearly understood. Yet our progress in practice will depend very much on our growing insight into theory.

As our personality develops we become less and less at the mercy of our immediate surroundings and the ways in which they affect us, and become more and more able to choose and create our surroundings and to plan ahead, often over long periods of time, for the things we want. Amongst other things, this means that we have to learn to think in an abstract way, to exercise our imagination and to consider things other than just our immediate sensations and desires. Only when he has reached this stage is the individual able to control his wish of the moment in the interests of his own more fundamental long-term needs. One expects a child of three, or even five, to run into the road and seek his ball – at those ages he is still largely at the mercy of the immediate situation. As he grows older, however, he is expected to take more things into account and to think ahead. By ten or eleven he is capable of pursuing goals some months distant in time. At sixteen or eighteen the more developed boy or girl is able to perform great feats of abstraction in time and space. This is the process whereby the individual frees himself from slavery to his instincts and the urge for immediate pleasure, and develops mental processes more adapted to the demands of the environment.

In the course of this process we develop within ourselves ways of harmonizing our different, and often conflicting, desires and learn to seek their satisfaction in the world outside ourselves: we begin to judge between the things we want in the future, to consider what things we desire most, to realize that some wishes have to give way to others, so that our actions may have purpose and may not clash in a haphazard way. Because one of our foremost long-term desires is to remain on friendly and cooperative terms with others we must keep their requirements firmly in the front of our minds: from this awareness of the things which please and displease the people round us come the rudiments of conscience.

In infancy and early childhood we are not able to act in this thoughtful way with regard to getting our own ends or to recognizing the claims of other people. During this time his mother has to act for a child in both these ways. She arranges where he shall be, when he shall feed and sleep and be washed, provides for him in every way, allows him to do some things, checks him in others. She is, as it were, his personality and his conscience. Gradually he learns these arts for himself, and, as he does so, the skilled parent transfers the roles to him. This is a slow, subtle, and continuous process, beginning when he first learns to walk and feed himself and not ending completely until maturity is reached. But the unfolding of the child's self and conscience can only go on satisfactorily when his first human relationships are continuous and happy.

Here we are struck by a similarity between this process and the development of the unborn child during the time while tissues, which do not yet show the characters of the different parts of the future baby, take on these characters under the influence of certain chemicals called organizers. If growth is to proceed smoothly, the tissues must be exposed to the influence of the appropriate organizer at certain critical periods. In the same way, if mental development is to proceed smoothly, it would appear to be necessary for the unformed mentality to be exposed, during certain critical periods, to the influence of a psychic organizer – the mother. For this reason, in considering the disorders to which personality and conscience are liable, it is imperative to have regard to the phases of development of the child's capacity for human relationships. These are many and naturally merge into one another. In broad outline, the following are the most important:

(*a*) The phase during which the infant is in course of establishing a relation with a clearly identified person – his mother; this is normally achieved by five or six months of age.

(*b*) The phase during which he needs her as an ever-present companion; this usually continues until about his third birthday.

(*c*) The phase during which he is becoming able to maintain a relationship with her in her absence. During the fourth and fifth years such a relationship can only be maintained in favourable circumstances and for a few days or weeks at a time; after seven or eight the relationship can be maintained, though not without strain, for periods of a year or more.

The ages by which these phases are completed no doubt vary greatly from child to child in the same way that the stages of physical maturity vary. For instance, the capacity to walk matures at any time between nine and twenty-four months, and it may well be that psychic growth is equally variable. If this is so, it will be wise in research to reckon age rather by the stage of development reached than by actual length of life, since it seems fairly certain that the kind and degree of psychological disorder following deprivation depends on the phase of development a child is in at the time. In putting forward this theory well-established principles gained from the study of embryos are again followed. We learn that abnormalities are produced by attacking, at just the right time, a region in which profound growth activity is under way. . . . Possible abnormalities will tend to fall into classes and types corresponding to the most critical stages and regions in development. Injuries inflicted early will in general produce widespread disturbances of growth . . . late injuries will tend on the other hand to produce local defects.

Furthermore,

a given undifferentiated tissue can respond to an organizer only during a limited period. It must have reached a certain stage of differentiation before it can respond; and later its character becomes fixed, so that it can yield only a more limited type of response.

In the same way a mother by her mere presence and tenderness can act as an 'organizer' on the mind of a child, still in the quite undeveloped stages of very early growth. But the time when this action can take place is, as in the case of the chemical 'organizer', limited to the time whilst the child's personality is quite unformed (this, of course, is quite a different matter from the continuing influence of the mother upon the child later). The evidence is fairly clear that if the first phase of development – that of establishing a relation with one particular person recognized as such – is not satisfactorily completed during the first twelve months or so, there is the greatest difficulty in making it good: the character of the psychic tissue has become fixed. (The limit for many children may well be a good deal earlier.) Similarly, there appears to be a limit by which the second and third phases must be completed if further development is to proceed. Now it is these vital growth processes which are impaired by the experience of deprivation. Observations of severely deprived children show that their personalities and their consciences are not developed – their behaviour is impulsive and uncontrolled and they are unable to pursue long-term goals because they are the victims of the momentary whim. For them, all wishes are born equal and equally to be acted upon. Their power of checking themselves is absent or feeble; and without this people cannot find their way efficiently about the world – they are swayed this way and that by every impulse. They are thus ineffective personalities unable to learn from experience, and consequently their own worst enemies. We cannot yet explain exactly how the deprivation of a mother's care produces this result, but two of the observations which have already been noticed may carry us some way towards understanding the problem. These are, first, Dr Goldfarb's discovery of the difficulty which these patients have in abstract thinking, of dealing with ideas rather than being tied to the objects immediately present to the senses; and second, the observation of doctors trying to help them of their being unable to come out of themselves through affection for other people or interest in things outside themselves.

All the institution children studied by Dr Goldfarb showed serious and special incapacity for abstract thinking. Now we have just seen that such thinking is necessary to the action of the self and of the conscience – the baby must gradually learn to think before he acts and to give up responding automatically to every happening, a sound, a light, hunger, or pain: only then can he become a full person. So it may well be that where abstract thinking has not developed properly the personality cannot fully unfold. But even so, there remains the puzzle as to why deprivation should injure the power of abstract thinking.

The failure of personality development in deprived children is perhaps more easily understood when it is considered that it is the mother who in a child's earliest years acts as his personality and his conscience. The institution children had never had this experience, and so had never had the opportunity of completing the first phase of development – that of establishing a relationship with a clearly known mother-figure. All they had had was a succession of makeshift agents each helping them in some limited way, but none providing continuity in time, which is of the essence of personality. It may well be that these grossly deprived infants, never having been the continuous objects of care of a single human being, had never had the opportunity to learn the processes of abstraction and of the organization of behaviour in time and space. Certainly their grave psychical deformities are clear examples of the principle that injuries inflicted early produce widespread disturbances of growth.

In the institutional setting, moreover, there is less opportunity for a child who has learnt how to think to exercise this art. In a family a young child is within limits encouraged to express himself both socially and in play. A child of eighteen months or two years has already become a character in the family. It is known that he enjoys certain things and dislikes others, and the family has learnt to respect his wishes. Furthermore, he is getting to know how to induce his parents or his brothers and sisters to do what he wants. In this way he is learning to change his social environment to a shape more congenial to him. The same occurs in his play, where in a symbolic way he is creating and recreating new worlds for himself. Here are the exercise grounds for personality. In any institutional setting much of this is lost; in the less good it may all be lost. The child is not encouraged to individual activity because it is a nuisance; it is easier if he stays put and does what he is told. Even if he strives to change his environment he fails. Toys are lacking: sometimes the children sit inert or rock themselves for hours together. Above all, the brief intimate games which mother and baby invent to amuse themselves as an accompaniment to getting up and washing, dressing, feeding, bathing, and returning to sleep – they are all missing. In these conditions, a child has no opportunity of learning and practising functions which are as basic to living as walking and talking.

The case of a child who has a good relation with his mother for a year or two and then suffers deprivation may be rather different. He has passed through the first phase of social development, that of establishing a relationship, and the shock affects the second phase in which, though personality development is proceeding apace, a child is still strongly attached to his mother, to whom he looks constantly for help and security. Only if she is with him or near at hand does he feel secure and so able to explore his surroundings and take an active part in life. If he is suddenly removed from her, to hospital or institution, he is faced with a situation in which he feels terrified and with tasks which he feels to be impossible. In a situation of this kind it is usual for such skill as has already been learnt to be lost. In these circumstances children often go back to more babyish ways of thinking and behaving and find it very difficult to grow out of them again.

A further principle of the theory of learning is that an individual cannot learn a skill unless he has a friendly feeling towards his teacher, and is ready to identify himself with her. Now this positive attitude towards his mother is either lacking in a deprived child, or, if present, is mixed with keen resentment. How early in a child's life deprivation causes a definitely hostile attitude is debatable, but it is certainly evident for all to see in the second year. No observation is more common than that of the child separated for a few weeks or months during the second, third, or fourth years failing to recognize his mother on reunion. It seems probable that this is sometimes a true failure to recognize, based on a loss of the capacity to abstract and identify. At others, it is certain that it is a refusal to recognize, since the children, instead of treating their parents as though they were strangers, are deliberate in their avoidance of them. The parents have become hated people. This hostility is variously expressed. It may take the form of tempers and violence; in older children it may be expressed in words. All who have treated such children are familiar with the violence of their fantasies against the parents whom they feel to have deserted them. Such an attitude not only is incompatible with their desire for love and security, and results in acute conflicts, anxiety, and depression, but is clearly a hindrance to their future social learning. So far from idolizing their parents and wishing to become like them, one side of their nature hates them and wishes to avoid having anything to do with them. This is what brings about aggressively bad or delinquent behaviour; it may also lead ultimately to suicide which is an alternative to murdering his parents.

In other cases a child has suffered so much pain through making relationships and having them interrupted that he is reluctant ever again to give his heart to anyone for fear of its being broken. And not only his own heart: he is afraid, too, to break the heart of new persons whom he might love because he might also vent his anger on them. Older children are sometimes aware of this and will remark to a psychiatrist: 'We had better not become too familiar, for I'm afraid I'll get angry with you then.' It is feelings such as these which underlie a child's shutting into himself. To withdraw from human contact is to avoid further frustrations and to avoid the intense depression which human beings experience as a result of hating the person whom they most dearly love and need. Withdrawal is thus felt to be the better of two bad alternatives. Unfortunately, it proves to be a blind alley, since no further development is then possible. For progress in human relations the individual must take the other road, in which he learns to tolerate his contradictory feelings and to bear the anxiety and depression which go with them. But experience show that once a person has taken refuge in the relative painlessness of withdrawal he is reluctant to change course and to risk the turmoil of feeling and misery which attempting relationships brings with it. As a result he loses his capacity to make affectionate relationships and to identify himself with loved people, and any treatment offered is resisted. Thenceforward he becomes a lone wolf, pursuing his ends irrespective of others. But his desire for love, repressed though it is, persists, resulting in behaviour such as promiscuous sex relations and the stealing of other people's possessions. Feelings of revenge also smoulder on, leading to other anti-social acts, sometimes of a very violent character.

Deprivation after the age of three or four, namely in the third phase, does not have the same destructive effect on personality development and on the ability for abstract thinking. It still results, however, in excessive desires for affection and excessive impulses for revenge, which cause acute internal conflict and unhappiness and very unfavourable social attitudes.

In both the second and third phases a child's restricted sense of time and his tendency to misunderstand a situation add greatly to his difficulties. It is exceedingly difficult for grown-ups to remember that a young child's grasp of time is meagre. A child of three can recall the events of a few days ago and anticipate those of a day or two hence. Notions such as last week or last month, next week or next month are incomprehensible. Even for a child of five or six, weeks are immensely long and months almost timeless. This very restricted time-span has to be understood if the despair which a young child feels at being left alone in a strange place is to be fully realized. Though to his mother it may seem not only a finite but relatively brief time, to him it is an eternity. It is this inability to imagine a time of deliverance which, together with a sense of helplessness, accounts for the overwhelming nature of his anxiety and despair. Perhaps the nearest to it a grown-up can conceive is to imagine being committed to prison on an indeterminate sentence.

This comparison is a good one, since the notion of punishment is itself not far from many a child's mind as the explanation of events. All psychiatrists have come across children who have seriously believed that their being sent away from home was to punish them for being naughty, a misconstruction which is often made even more terrifying and distressing by being unexpressed. At other times children imagine that it has been their fault that the home has been broken up. Commonly there is bewilderment and perplexity regarding the course of events, which leads a child to be unable to accept and respond to his new environment and the new people caring for him. Naturally a child who has suffered gross privation in early infancy, or who for other reasons cannot make relationships, will not be affected in these ways, but will greet each change with genial indifference. But for a child who has had opportunity to make relationships it is not so easy to change loyalties. Indeed, very many of the problems which arise as a result of moving an older child to a foster-home are caused by a failure to recognize the deep attachment which a child has for his parents, even if they are exceedingly bad and have given him little affection. Unless these perplexities are cleared up and these loyalties respected, a child will remain anchored in an unsatisfactory past, endlessly trying to find his mother and refusing to adapt to the new situation and make the best of it. This results in a dissatisfied restless character unable to make either himself or anyone else happy.

CHAPTER 6

Methods of Research

IT is now demonstrated that maternal care in infancy and early childhood is essential for mental health. This is a discovery of which the importance may be compared to that of the role of vitamins in physical health, and is of far-reaching significance for the prevention of mental ill-health. On this new understanding social measures of great consequence for the future will be based. These measures will be wisely planned, however, only if knowledge of what is essential and what is not is progressively increased.

Not only is further research in the field necessary to guide immediate preventive measures, but it promises also to cast light on some of the fundamental problems of personality development, on the understanding of which all the social sciences depend. Personality growth is the result of an interaction between the growing organism and other human beings. In some way the individual takes in, and so grows to resemble, his social surroundings, though he always remains himself: he is never like any other product of the community. How this process of becoming like one's surroundings proceeds is not understood. It is severely upset by deprivation in infancy and early childhood, and in the history of medicine it has often been the study of wrong functioning which has most clearly illuminated the nature of the function itself. It may well be that in studying these serious failures to fit into the social group a clearer light will be thrown on the ways in which personality grows. Whether research in this field is undertaken to improve our fundamental knowledge or to guide our measures to prevent damage to children, henceforward it should not be necessary to spend time in proving the harmfulness of deprivation. Research workers should be encouraged to move on, both to the study of what actually happens and to recognizing and unravelling the effects of the many different forces at work. Though aware of some of them – age and emotional development of the child, length of deprivation, degree of deprivation, relations with mother-figure before and after deprivation – there are, no doubt, others of which we are still ignorant. Matters of immediate practical significance on which information is needed are the lengths of the safety margin (*a*) during which deprivation can, if absolutely necessary, be permitted, and (*b*) within which there is time to make good damage already done.

As the last chapter showed, investigators are still far from clear as to the way in which the mind absorbs from without the things by which it grows. Even so, we can make guesses as to how these things happen and put these guesses, or theories, into clear form so that they can be tested. The method of research must always be first to make such theories and then by observations to test whether they are true or not. But even when we have our theories clearly stated there are immense problems as to how to test them.

In the first place, it is not possible cold-bloodedly to arrange for children to be deprived of mothering at various ages and for varying periods. The investigator is very largely dependent on his discovering groups of children who, for one reason or another, are being or have been subject to this experience. Ideally, to make sure one is dealing only with the effects of separation, all other factors known to be emotionally disturbing would be absent from the cases. Thus the ideal sample would consist of healthy children of good parentage, who, so long as they were with their mothers, would have enjoyed good relationships with them. The reason for separation, moreover, would not be harmful in itself, while the conditions obtaining during separation would be carefully regulated. In practice, few of these ideal research conditions hold. Deprived children are often sick and many are born of unstable or defective parents. Family relationships while they last leave much to be desired, and the home is commonly broken up because of destitution, neglect, or death. Many of the children are illegitimate and unwanted. Psychological conditions in institutions or foster-homes cannot easily be arranged to suit the research worker.

A further major difficulty is that of getting permission to study the cases. Detailed studies of infants in their homes and of their relations to their mothers require a degree of intimate contact not often permitted to the professional observer. Even when these infants are in institutions, the feelings of the workers who are caring for them may make scientific study difficult. Finally, parents who are anxious and guilty about their children's later behaviour may resent further inquiry.

There are no simple ways round these difficulties. It is far better, however, to study a fairly small number of children about whom full and accurate information can be had than to try to make elaborate statistical comparisons with large numbers in our knowledge of whom there are many gaps. The best answers will probably be got by studying small groups of children, carefully 'matched' so that they are as much alike in their circumstances as possible, apart from the one fact of separation. To regulate the child's experiences while in an institution is more difficult, though, in the main, it will be possible to select places where far-seeing attempts are being made to provide substitute care and others where such attempts are not being made. Variables which are more difficult to control are the length of time a child is in an institution and what happens to him afterwards. Suffice it to say that only planned investigations of numbers of very carefully selected cases are likely to unravel the influences of all these variables.

The problem of access – how to get at a group of people or children to study them – is always present when psychologists seek to make studies of human beings which try to go beyond a superficial description of behaviour to its inner springs; this is so because people habitually hide many of their feelings, especially those about which they are anxious or guilty. The only key yet found to unlock these secrets is the approach in which the research worker holds himself in readiness to help his subjects by treatment should they wish it. Naturally many will not respond, but others, sensing that the research worker is ready to aid them as well as to study them, will give him opportunities for both.

Fortunately, the matter is much easier if we use animals as our experimental subjects, as Professor Liddell has done at Cornell University. He has studied goats, but it may be that dogs, which are being studied in a research station in the State of Maine, U.S.A., will prove more rewarding subjects, since much of a practical kind is already known about their social development. For instance, it is a commonplace that a sporting dog must be trained by one master, who must feed him himself, and that there are difficulties in transfer to a new master. Starting with the knowledge already available, it should be relatively easy to construct a series of experiments and perhaps gain insights which could then be tested with human beings.

A research team working on these problems, whether with animals or human beings, and preferably with both, needs to bring many methods to their joint task. The only way of making sure that all the necessary information is likely to be obtained in the end is by comparing the facts learned by one method with those learned in other ways.

The doctor and the experimental scientist must work together. It is usually the doctor who has the earliest insight, defines the problem, and makes the first theories. He knows in detail the feelings and motives of his patients and the complicated intellectual and emotional stresses to which they give rise; he has information about the relations between his patients' mental life and their experiences which no one else can give. He provides the first sketch-map which, though it needs correction in many particulars, gives an invaluable overall picture of the new territory: it is no accident that psychiatrists and others closely associated with them played a leading part in bringing to light the bad effects of maternal deprivation.

But following the doctor actually treating patients must come other scientific workers who will study in more detail how far the actual observations confirm the theories proposed. Their work again may lead to fresh theories, which again must be tested by experiment and observation. Surveys and statistical work must be planned and carried out, using all the insight the practising psychiatrist can supply. On his side the psychiatrist must select for further study just those cases which the statistically trained worker considers likely to give most understanding of the problem.

Besides the use of all psychological methods, there is good reason to include some types of physical measurements. For example, systematic recording of changes of height and weight will probably be important. So too will the study of graphs, which can now be made by a machine showing the rhythmic electrical discharges from the brain itself. It has commonly been supposed that where these rhythms show abnormality the cause is some defect of the brain present before birth or caused by physical injury, but it may prove that they can also result from early psychological experiences influencing the way the brain itself develops.

Clearly then here, in the embryology of personality, is a field rich and ripe for research and one to be exploited to the full before increasingly effective methods of prevention have made such cases rare and so difficult to study. At first an individual reacts to the outside world by vague large reactions not precisely directed, but as he grows and gets to know what he wants his reactions are more purposeful and more precise, and so more effective (compare the blundering way in which a baby waves his arms towards something that attracts his notice and the accurate movements of a surgeon). In the same way in his search for clearer understanding and more fitting action the scientist moves on from the observation of some large general relationship to a finer and finer appreciation of the nature of the forces at work and of their influence on each other. In the field of mental health and its relation to maternal care investigators have so far done no more than perceive these large scale relationships. It is for workers of the coming half-century to observe more exactly, to detect all the influences at work and to unravel how they relate to each other, and so to give the power to prevent mental illness.

Part II

PREVENTION OF MATERNAL DEPRIVATION

CHAPTER 7

The Purpose of the Family

THE demonstration that maternal deprivation in the early years has a bad effect on personality growth is a challenge to action. How can this deprivation be prevented so that children may grow up mentally healthy?

It was said at the beginning of the first chapter that what is believed to be essential for mental health is that the infant and young child should experience a warm, intimate, and continuous relationship with his mother (or mother-substitute), in which both find satisfaction and enjoyment. A child needs to feel he is an object of pleasure and pride to his mother; a mother needs to feel an expansion of her own personality in the personality of her child: each needs to feel closely identified with the other. The mothering of a child is not something which can be arranged by rota; it is a live human relationship which alters the characters of both partners. The provision of a proper diet calls for more than calories and vitamins: we need to enjoy our food if it is to do us good. In the same way, the provision of mothering cannot be considered in terms of hours per day, but only in terms of the enjoyment of each other's company which mother and child obtain.

Such enjoyment and close identification of feeling is possible for either party only if the relationship is continuous. Much emphasis has already been laid on the necessity of continuity for the growth of a child's personality. It should be remembered, too, that continuity is necessary for the growth of a mother. Just as a baby needs to feel that he belongs to his mother, a mother needs to feel that she belongs to her child, and it is only when she has the satisfaction of this feeling that it is easy for her to devote herself to him. The provision of constant attention night and day, seven days a week and 365 days in the year, is possible only for a woman who derives profound satisfaction from seeing her child grow from babyhood, through the many phases of childhood, to become an independent man or woman, and knows that it is her care which has made this possible.

It is for these reasons that the mother-love which a young child needs is so easily provided within the family, and is so very very difficult to provide outside it. The services which mothers and fathers habitually render their children are so taken for granted that their greatness is forgotten. In no other relationship do human beings place themselves so unreservedly and so continuously at the disposal of others. This holds true even of bad parents – a fact far too easily forgotten by their critics, especially critics who have never had the care of children of their own. It must never be forgotten that even a bad parent who neglects her child is none-the-less providing much for him. Except in the worst cases, she is giving him food and shelter, comforting him in distress, teaching him simple skills, and above all is providing him with that continuity of human care on which his sense of security rests. He may be ill-fed and ill-sheltered, he may be very dirty and suffering from disease, he may be ill-treated, but, unless his parents have wholly rejected him, he is secure in the knowledge that there is someone to whom he is of value and who will strive, even though inadequately, to provide for him until such time as he can fend for himself.

It is against this background that the reason why young children thrive better in bad homes than in good institutions, and why children with bad parents are, apparently unreasonably, so attached to them, can be understood. Those responsible for institutions have sometimes been unwilling to acknowledge that children are often better off in even quite bad homes, which is the conclusion of most experienced social workers with mental health training and is borne out by evidence already quoted. It will be remembered that when a group of children, aged between one and four years, who had spent their lives in institutions was compared with a similar group who lived in their, often very unsatisfactory, homes and spent the day in day-nurseries because their mothers were working, the difference in development was much in favour of the children living at home and attending day-nursery. In another follow-up study, comparing the social adjustment in adult life of children who spent five years or more of their childhood in institutions with others who had spent the same years at home (in 80 per cent of cases in bad homes), the results were clearly in favour of the bad homes, those growing up to be socially incapable being only about half (18 per cent) of those from institutions (34·5 per cent).

That one-third of all those who had spent five years or more of their lives in institutions turned out to be 'socially incapable' in adult life is alarming, and no less alarming in the light of the reflection that one of the principal social functions of an adult is that of parenthood. For one may be reasonably sure that all the 34 per cent of these institution children who grew up to be 'socially incapable' adults were incapable as parents, and one may suspect that some at least of those who were not grossly incapable socially still left much to be desired as parents. Yet, incapable as parents though they may have been, it is unlikely that they were childless. On the contrary, many must have had children and many of these children must have been neglected and deprived. Thus it is seen how children who suffer deprivation grow up to become parents lacking the capacity to care for their children, and how adults lacking this capacity are commonly those who suffered deprivation in childhood. This vicious circle is the most serious aspect of the problem and one to which this book will constantly revert.

Naturally this evidence that bad homes are often better than good institutions is far from final, and in any case all depends on how bad is the home and how good the institution. Nevertheless, it serves as a reminder that there may be something worse than a bad home – and that is no home. As Sir James Spence has pointed out in his inspiring lecture, carrying a title which has been borrowed to name this chapter, one of the principal purposes of the family is the preservation of the art of parenthood. Unless this art is preserved, a function as necessary to the preservation of society as the production of food will fall into decay. Yet the merits of particular methods of child upbringing are rarely judged by the performance as parents of the children they rear; in particular, this standard seems never to have been applied to measure the success or failure of methods at present used for the care of children deprived of a normal home life.

The attachment of children to parents who, by all ordinary standards, are very bad is a never-ceasing source of wonder to those who seek to help them. Even when they are with kindly foster-parents these children feel their roots to be in the homes where, perhaps, they have been neglected and ill-treated, and keenly resent criticisms directed against their parents. Efforts made to 'save' a child from his bad surroundings and to give him new standards are commonly of no avail, since it is his own parents who, for good or ill, he values and with whom he is identified. (This is a fact of critical importance when considering how best to help children who are living in intolerable conditions.) These sentiments are not surprising when it is remembered that, despite much neglect, one or other parent has almost always and in countless ways been kind to him from the day of his birth onwards, and, however much the outsider sees to criticize, the child sees much to be grateful for. At least his mother has cared for him after a fashion all his life, and not until someone else has shown herself equally or more dependable has he reason to trust her. Unfortunately, he is usually right in his mistrust. Once a child is out of his own home he is lucky if he finds someone who will care for him till he is grown up. Even for good organizations the rate at which children have to be shifted from foster-home to foster-home is deplorably high; even in good institutions the turnover of staff is a constant problem. However devoted foster-parents or house-mothers may be, they have not the same sense of absolute obligation to a child which all but the worst parents possess. When other interests and duties call, a foster-child takes second place. A child is therefore right to distrust them – from his point of view there is no one like his own parents.

This conclusion was reached by the British Ministry of Health in its survey of the lessons of evacuating children from the dangers of bombing during the Second World War:

> One point which all experience in the evacuation scheme has emphasized is the importance of the family in a child's development and the impossibility of providing children with any completely adequate substitute for the care of their own parents. This has led to an increased awareness in some quarters of the importance of improving home conditions in order to keep families together instead of removing children from unsatisfactory homes.

A warning that the decision to remove a child from his own home is one of great gravity was given many years ago by a distinguished quartet of American psychiatrists and social workers:

> The decision which for any cause separates a child from his family is very serious; it sets in motion events which to a greater or lesser degree affect the whole of his future life. Whether the removal is due to sickness, neglect, desertion, inefficiency, or death of parents, or to the child's conduct inside or outside the home, the transfer to the control of strangers should not be made without much forethought. . . . Too often children are taken from their families with very little, if any, study of the causes that lie behind the situation. Many agencies mistakenly approach the problem with predetermined ideas of the conditions which would warrant removal rather than with the purpose of ascertaining whether the home of the parents can be made suitable for the child.

Though this was written many years ago, its message is as timely today as it was then. It is still common in Western communities to see in the removal of a child from home the solution to many a family problem, without there being any appreciation of the gravity of the step and, often, without there being any clear plan for the future. It is too often forgotten that in removing a child of five from home direct responsibility is taken for his future health and happiness for a decade to come, and that in removing an infant the crippling of his character is at risk.

From all this the trite conclusion is reached that family life is of pre-eminent importance and that 'there's no place like home'. But, trite though it may be, its truth is often flouted and, judging by the meagre and confused literature on the subject, little attention has been given to the conditions making for family prosperity and family decay. Since the basic method of preventing a child suffering maternal deprivation must be to ensure that he receives nurture within his own family, it is necessary to consider these matters in some detail. This is a departure from the tradition set by reports on deprived children, which have given scant attention to methods by which home conditions may be improved so that families may remain together, and which have, instead, hurried on to consider how best to arrange for their care elsewhere. On this topic a great literature of reports and textbooks has grown up, all assuming that homeless children are an inevitable feature of social life and most of them content to discuss their care without reference to the reasons for which they come into care. It must, of course, be recognized that on occasion children have to be cared for outside their own homes, but let such arrangements be regarded as a last resort to be undertaken only when it is absolutely impossible for the home to be made fit for the child.

Three linked circumstances in which a child suffers maternal deprivation may be distinguished:

(*a*) The partial deprivation of living with a mother or permanent mother-substitute, including a relative, whose attitude towards him is unfavourable;

(*b*) The complete deprivation of losing his mother (or

permanent mother-substitute) by death, illness, or desertion and having no familiar relatives to care for him;

(*c*) The complete deprivation of being removed from his mother (or permanent mother-substitute) to strangers by courts of law or by medical or social agencies, including voluntary societies.

Naturally cases coming under (*a*) above are very numerous and of all degrees of severity, from the child whose mother leaves him to scream for many hours because the baby-books tell her to do so, to infants whose mothers wholly reject them. The partial forms of maternal deprivation, due sometimes to ignorance, but more often to unconscious hostility on the part of the mother growing out of experiences in her own childhood, could well form the subject of another book. Many child-guidance workers believe they make up a large fraction of all the cases they are called upon to treat, and that the process of helping a mother to appreciate her true feelings for her child and their origins in her own childhood is an essential part of child guidance. However, this book has for its purpose the consideration of the more obvious forms of deprivation, and it is to the prevention of these that attention will be given. The great majority of them are the result of family failure, and for this reason the focus will be on cases where the child never had a family, where his family has broken down, or where social agencies have removed him from his home because it has been judged to have failed. However, in addition to these, there is a sufficient number of cases where, owing to maladjustment or physical illness, children are removed from home by medical or legal authorities, and are thus deprived of maternal care, for it to be necessary to give them some separate consideration, even though it is not infrequent for these conditions themselves to be the result of family failure.

CHAPTER 8

Why do Families Fail?

DEFINITIONS which attempt to describe 'normal home life' in terms of family structure are seen to be inadequate. Not only is it clear that a child can have a normal home life when living with relatives other than his parents, but it is obvious that a child can be living with his own parents and yet not be getting a normal home life. It is evident that the definition must be in terms of what actually happens to the child.

It is because a young child is not an organism capable of independent life that he requires a special social institution to aid him during his period of immaturity. This social institution must aid him in two ways: first, by helping in the satisfaction of immediate animal needs such as nutrition, warmth, and shelter, and protection from danger; secondly, by providing surroundings in which he may develop his physical, mental, and social capacities to the full so that, when grown up, he may be able to deal with his physical and social environment effectively. This demands an atmosphere of affection and security.

Traditions as to who normally performs these indispensable functions of child care vary from community to community. In most, the child's natural mother and father play leading parts, though even this is not always the case. Traditions vary, especially in regard to the extent to which there are accepted substitutes for mother and father readily available. In many of the economically less-developed communities, people live in large family groups made up of three or four generations. Near and known relatives – grandmothers, aunts, older sisters – are thus always at hand to take the maternal role in an emergency. Economic support, moreover, is forthcoming if the breadwinner is incapacitated. The greater family group living together in one locality provides a social insurance system of great value. Even in Western communities, there are many rural and urban pockets in which close-knit and much intermarried village groups provide similar social services for their members. It is probably only in communities in which the greater family group has ceased to exist that the problem of deprived children is found on a serious scale. This condition is found in many communities of Western industrialized culture, in which it is usual for young men and women to migrate far from their birthplace and, not infrequently, to move many times in the course of their married lives. As a result of such migrations very many families have such loose ties with their local surroundings that for whole communities it has ceased to be a tradition to help a neighbour in distress. As a result of this social break-up a far heavier responsibility for child care is placed on the father and mother than is the case in more traditional close-knit communities. Not only does such a broken-up community provide no substitutes should a mother or father be temporarily or permanently incapacitated but, by putting this great load on parents, it may destroy a family which in better circumstances could hold together.

In Western communities today it is the tradition that 'normal home life' is provided by a child's mother and father, which is conveniently described as the child's 'natural home group'. Despite social break-up, it still remains the tradition (though less strong than formerly) that, if this group fails for any reason, near relatives take responsibility for the child. In any analysis of the causes of children becoming deprived, therefore, it has to be considered not only why the natural home group has failed, but also why relatives have failed to act as substitutes.

CAUSES OF THE NATURAL HOME GROUP FAILING TO CARE FOR A CHILD

These are conveniently grouped under three heads according to the state of the natural home group:

(1) Natural home group never established:
- Illegitimacy.

(2) Natural home group intact, but not functioning effectively:
- Economic conditions leading to unemployment of breadwinner with consequent poverty.
- Chronic illness or incapacity of parent.
- Instability or mental unfitness of parent.

(3) Natural home group broken up and therefore not functioning:
- Social calamity – war, famine.
- Death of a parent.
- Illness requiring hospitalization of a parent.
- Imprisonment of a parent.
- Desertion by one or both parents.
- Separation or divorce.
- Employment of father elsewhere.
- Full-time employment of mother.

Any family suffering from one or more of these conditions must be regarded as a possible source of deprived children. Whether or not these children actually become deprived will depend on (*a*) whether both or only one parent is affected; (*b*) whether, if only one parent is affected, help is given to the other; and (*c*) whether relatives or neighbours are able and willing to act as substitutes. All these points must be considered, and information on them got for a case to be properly understood.

It is at present impossible to obtain even reasonably satisfactory figures giving the proportions of children deprived of a normal home life on account of these different conditions and of combinations of them. The obscurity is particularly notable in the second group where the natural home group is still in existence, but for some reason not working effectively. Terms such as sloth, neglect, destitution, lack of parental control, and cruelty are used, which do little more than describe the symptoms of the failure without in any way accounting for it. Notes of the factors responsible for such conditions, especially ill-health and mental instability, both of which are now known to be of great importance, are conspicuous by their absence. Similarly, under the third heading, death of a parent or desertion is frequently regarded as sufficient without even stating whether it is the father or the mother who has died or deserted, let alone the circumstances preventing the other caring for the child. It is very much to be hoped that it may in future be possible to design more adequate lists of the causes of deprivation and of relatives failing to act as substitutes, and so to collect figures which are at once informative and comparable with others.

It is not possible in this book to attempt a thorough survey of whatever statistics exist. To obtain some idea of the proportions of the problem, however, certain figures which happened to be easily available have been taken account of from the United Kingdom, the U.S.A. and Sweden. The main conclusions to be drawn from them, and from discussions with experienced social workers, are as follows:

(*a*) The death of one or both parents is no longer of overriding importance, largely because fewer adults of childbearing age now die and there are schemes of assistance for widows with children. Such cases probably account for less than 25 per cent of all cases. In two of the largest samples, one British and the other American, the percentages were 10 and 6 respectively.

(*b*) Illegitimacy features prominently in all sets of figures, varying from about 10 per cent to 40 per cent. In homes for infants and children under six in Denmark in about 1945 the percentage was 80.

(*c*) The natural home group being existent but not functioning effectively, resulting in 'neglect', 'destitution', 'lack of parental control', or 'maladjustment of child', is prominent in all but one set of figures and shows this condition to be the greatest single cause today. Poverty, neglect, and lack of parental control account for 60 per cent of cases in one large British sample, while maladjustment of the child is responsible for 26 per cent of cases in a New York sample.

(*d*) Where the natural home group is broken up, separation and divorce are common factors, varying from about 5 per cent to 25 per cent of all cases.

(*e*) Another important cause of the break-up of the natural home group is prolonged illness of a parent, necessitating his or her being sent to hospital (or, in the case of mental defectives, an institution). Mental illness and defect are the most frequent and probably account for some 5 per cent to 10 per cent of all cases.

(*f*) A situation has arisen in the United Kingdom in which is is legally possible for parents who have been evicted for not paying their rent to leave the children in the care of a local authority and to find accommodation for themselves where children are not accepted. In one area this accounts for about 33 per cent of the children in care.

Most of these immediate causes of children needing care have hitherto been accepted fatalistically as an inevitable part of social life, and until recent years no attempt was made to look beyond them into the underlying factors at work. Are illegitimacy, neglect, maladjustment, and desertion to be accepted as unavoidable social evils, or is there some prospect of understanding the forces promoting them and of combating them? It is the argument of this book that the present increased knowledge of human nature and of the part which family life plays in its developing gives many and valuable clues to the understanding of the forces at work. All these forces can be grouped broadly under the headings economic, social, and medical: the *economic* contain the opportunities, or lack of opportunities, the family has for earning an adequate livelihood; the *social*, the social system within which it lives and which provides greater or less support; and the *medical*, the mental and physical health of the parents which determine what use is made of the opportunities offered. It is at once evident that which of these three sets of forces is the most important will vary enormously from one community to another and, in the same community, from one period to another. Sometimes the economic forces will be stronger, sometimes the social or the medical, and at all times they will interact. No attempt is made here to discuss the economic forces at work. In what follows an attempt has been made to explore the nature and effect of the social and medical forces and to give special attention to psychiatric factors.

There is no group of children in danger of deprivation in whose production psychiatric factors play a larger part than illegitimates. For this reason, and because the care of illegitimates raises special problems, a separate chapter has been given to them. The present chapter will be concerned with the psychiatric factors leading to the natural home group either breaking up or, although unbroken, failing to function effectively. Considering that personality disturbances, especially in mothers, almost certainly play the principal part in the majority of the cases coming into permanent care in Western communities today, it is remarkable that so little attention has hitherto been given to them. They are of particular importance in contributing to such differing conditions as neglect, cruelty, the prolonged ill-health of a parent, lack of parental control, unhappy marriage, desertion, separation, and divorce. Each of these will be discussed in turn, note being taken of the contributions to their origin of psychiatric disabilities in the parents and the part played by deprivation and unhappiness in the childhoods of those parents.

Neglect

Cases in which parents are deemed to be neglecting their children are of different kinds. Often the failure is in respect of physical care only and many experienced social workers have testified to the frequency with which children who have been 'neglected' in the sense of their being dirty and ill-nourished are in excellent mental health and have clearly not suffered from the deprivation of love. Unfortunately, so preoccupied with physical health, and, it might be added, physical appearance, have workers sometimes been that the paradox has been witnessed of expensive social action being taken to convert a physically neglected but psychologically well-provided child into a physically well-provided but emotionally starved one.

At least two forms of neglect can therefore be recognized – physical neglect and emotional neglect – and, though they may often coexist, it is of prime importance to distinguish them, since they need very different remedies. Broadly speaking, it will be found that, while *physical* neglect is most often due to economic factors, the ill-health of the mother, and ignorance, *emotional* neglect is the result of emotional instability and mental illness in the parents. Mental defect may contribute to both.

The causes of parents who are living together neglecting their children was the subject of a report published in 1948 by a group of English women under the chairmanship of the late Mrs Eva Hubback. While it suggests that in England in the years 1946–7 external and economic factors were not the principal cause, and that personal factors in the parents were of more substantial importance, it unfortunately failed to discuss these personal factors in much detail. Though the observations on which its conclusions are based are far from satisfactory, there is no evidence that too much attention was given to psychiatric factors – indeed the reverse is probably the case.

In this report external and economic factors are discussed

under four main headings, the principal conclusions being as follows:

Poverty: 'Insufficient income was not generally considered to be directly responsible for neglect in the larger number of cases', though 'complete inability . . . to manage the household budget . . . clearly may be a cause, and there were many examples of foolish spending'.

Size of family: 'Most witnesses were of the opinion that child-neglect in large families is no greater than in small', but 'there is abundant evidence . . . that pregnancies too close together' can undermine the mother's health.

Bad housing conditions: Though there can be no doubt that bad housing can make already existing difficulties worse, it was none the less reported that 'the homes where child-neglect was frequently found were not slum property nor poky hovels'.

Mother normally working: They found 'no conclusive evidence that this was a cause of neglect'.

In other Western communities it may well be that unemployment with inadequate insurance systems and consequent poverty are a major cause of a family going downhill, ultimately leading to neglect, but such conditions were apparently not common in England when this report was written. On the other hand, the report emphasizes the importance of physical and mental ill-health of the parents, both of which, it believes, have been greatly under-estimated in the past.

There is reason to believe that a wider study of women guilty of neglecting their children would confirm that not only do they not enjoy the kind of robust good health which would make their task possible, but that many would be in very poor health indeed. . . . There is . . . a widespread failure to recognize psychological factors. People look for bad housing, poverty, and overcrowding as reasons for neglect. Too seldom do they take into account emotional conflict or abnormality.

These are also the conclusions of the various medical officers of health who have investigated 'problem families', namely, families which exhibit a number of social problems, among which persistent child neglect is prominent, and which do not respond to ordinary measures of social aid. The parents in problem families, especially the mothers, are found frequently to be ineducable and unstable of character. Though mental defect is not infrequent (mental defect or near mental defect was found in about 25 per cent of the mothers of problem families, both in an urban and a rural district of England), it is agreed that this is not the major problem. Many borderline defectives make satisfactory parents if circumstances are reasonably favourable and familiar and they do not have too many children. On the other hand, a temperamental instability which expresses itself in fecklessness, irresponsibility, improvidence, and indiscipline in the home is often present in either or both parents, but commonly in the mother. With regard to the situation in the home, we read: 'There are no papers, no books, no clock or calendar or other things of rule or order. . . . There is no attempt at planning or saving. When money is obtained, it is immediately expended, often on expensive delicacies.' It is clearly this fundamental inability to consider matters other than those of the moment which accounts for their lack of response to education and other measures designed to help them. It seems that bad housing has very little to do with the problem – it is the ineducable maladjusted character which is the heart of it.

Apart from these unchanging character disorders, which may lead to gross neglect, are the passing conditions of anxiety and depression which, if present in a mother, may lead her to neglect her household duties, and result in the home gradually sinking into a slum. Her loving feelings for the children may cease or become infused with impatience and bitterness. Though such a condition is really an illness requiring medical attention, it frequently goes undiagnosed until the home has sunk below tolerable limits, in which circumstances it is more likely to be regarded as a social offence.

Discussions with social workers prominent in child care in the U.S.A. have again and again emphasized the importance of the emotional problems in the parents as being a major cause of children being in need of care, and have emphasized, too, the extent to which deprivation and unhappiness in the parents' own childhoods have been the cause of their present problems. The maladjusted and unstable parent met as the cause of child neglect is clearly as often as not the grown-up affectionless, maladjusted child, described earlier as one of the most unhappy products of maternal deprivation. Here again are the fickleness and irresponsibility, the inability to adopt an abstract attitude or to learn, the inaccessibility to help, the superficial relationships, the promiscuous sexual behaviour, with all of which the reader will have already become familiar. Admittedly, many such problem parents do not show all these features – in some the disability may be only partial – but it seems beyond doubt that they are at bottom the same thing. This social succession – of the neglected psychopathic child growing up to become the neglectful psychopathic parent – has hitherto received little attention: on the contrary, the impression is given that those investigating problem families have been more concerned with the possible inheritance of characteristics which might account for the maladjustment and fecklessness of parents than with the events of their early childhoods. Because research workers have not so far given attention to this aspect of the matter, well-authenticated facts are scarce. The main theory is borne out, however, by the analysis of 234 pairs of parents who had contributed 346 children to Dr Barnado's Homes in the years 1937–9. It is true that in 60 per cent of the mothers and 76 per cent of the fathers no information regarding the parents' background was available, but this in itself is an important pointer, because, as the investigators state: 'We have the impression that this type of parent has led an unsettled life, lacking permanent connexions, which makes a full case history impossible.' In the cases where it was possible to learn something of the parents' childhood it was found that 31 per cent of the fathers and as many as 58 per cent of the mothers had been deprived of a normal home life in their childhood. The majority were physically or mentally handicapped. Many of them appeared to have been either neglected or cruelly treated as children. These figures are not complete or exact, but they are not likely to err on the side of exaggerating the importance of these psychiatric troubles. It is hoped that in future research into problem families attention will be given to the upbringing of the parents themselves.

Physical Cruelty

Mercifully physical cruelty is rare, accounting for no more than 3 per cent to 5 per cent of children in care. Though no psychiatric study of the personalities and childhood histories of parents guilty of this behaviour seems to have been undertaken, psychiatrists' experience of schoolchildren referred on account of their cruel behaviour to others shows them to be suffering from severe maladjustment, almost always a result of gross deprivation or rejection. Cruelty to animals and other children is a characteristic, though not common, feature of the affectionless delinquent, and occasional outbursts of senseless cruelty are well known in some forms of mental illness. It is, therefore, probably safe to predict that when a study of parents guilty of physical cruelty to their children is made, personality disturbances will prove the rule, and that these will be found often to be the result of deprivation or rejection in childhood.

Prolonged Ill-health of a Parent

The contribution of chronic ill-health in a parent, especially the mother, to the causes of children becoming deprived has been much underrated in the past. Once again, moreover, attention must be called to psychiatric factors, since, as a leading American authority has stated, 'mental disease of a parent is one of the most common factors leading to child dependency' whether the mother is in a mental hospital or not. Because of its frequency and long duration, mental illness often plays an even larger part than physical illness in leading children to become in need of care; for not only does undiagnosed psychological ill-health in the mother underlie much neglect of children in their homes, but, when the condition is diagnosed, her prolonged convalescence or hospitalization may make special measures for their care elsewhere needful. It is unnecessary to repeat here the evidence pointing to unhappy childhood relationships as being a very important cause of mental unfitness.

Lack of Parental Control

In many countries legal machinery exists for removing children from their parents' care, either with or without parental consent, on the grounds of their being 'out of control'. Most such children are neglected, maladjusted, or both. Since it is often a matter of chance under which designation a child is dealt with and since in any case maladjustment and lack of parental control are but the two sides of a single coin, no separate consideration will be given to this heading. Maladjustment is dealt with in Chapter 14.

Unhappy Marriage, Desertion, Separation, and Divorce

Though a stable happy marriage is clearly necessary for the effective family care of children, comparatively little research has been undertaken into the influences which bring about such marriages. Two inquiries were carried out in the U.S.A. in the 1930s. They agree in finding three things to be of the greatest importance for married happiness: the married happiness of the couples' parents; happiness of childhood; no conflict with the mother. One pair of investigators analysed answers to questionnaires by 526 couples, mostly young middle-class Americans. From this part of their inquiry they conclude that the condition of their childhoods that was most relevant to the happiness of their marriages was the happiness or unhappiness of their parents' marriages. Next in importance came the degree of their affection for their own parents, particularly for their mothers. These research workers made a more detailed study of 100 couples. From it they came to the conclusion that the love-life of the grown person is conditioned by his love relationships during childhood. These conclusions, arrived at independently by psychologists and sociologists of high standing, must be taken as important evidence confirming the main propositions underlying this book and of the particular proposition of this chapter – that deprived and unhappy children grow up to make bad parents.

CAUSES OF RELATIVES FAILING TO ACT AS SUBSTITUTES

It has already been pointed out that it still remains the tradition in Western communities for near relatives to care for children when the natural home group has for any reason failed, and that no account of the causes of a particular child becoming homeless is complete unless the reason for relatives failing to act in this way is given. The usual reasons for failure are:

(*a*) Relatives dead, aged, or ill.
(*b*) Relatives living far away.
(*c*) Relatives unable to help for economic reasons.
(*d*) Relatives unwilling to help.
(*e*) The parents never had relatives (namely, were brought up in a series of foster-homes or an institution from early years).

It may well be that in present Western communities relatives are fewer and less available for emergency aid than formerly, owing to the combined effects of a lower birth-rate, the employment of women, and the breaking up of society. Even so, there are probably few families which have no relatives, and failure to help is likely often to be due to distance, lack of accommodation, or other economic difficulty. When this is so, wisely given material aid could in many cases keep the child within his greater family group.

The conditions giving rise to most difficulty fall under heads (*d*) and (*e*), where relatives are either unwilling to help or have never been available.

Not infrequently the state of affairs which causes the failure of the parents to provide for the child is also the cause of relatives being unwilling to substitute. For instance, the unmarried mother not only has difficulties economically, but may also be alienated from her relatives. The mental instability and maladjustment which frequently leads to poverty and neglect on the one hand, or to desertion on the other, is also likely to be associated with bad relations with relatives and neighbours. A Children's Officer writes: 'I always find out why the applicant cannot get help from relations and neighbours, and almost invariably it is because he himself is an unneighbourly person who has alienated the willingness of others to help.' Personality factors may thus play an important part in destroying both the first and second line of defence against 'homelessness'.

Those who are fortunate in belonging to large and united families are aware of the great sense of security they get from the knowledge that, should death suddenly overtake them, relatives willing to care for their children are certainly available. The absence of such a greater family is one of the many handicaps from which a child deprived of a normal home life suffers when he grows up and becomes a parent.

From the foregoing, it is evident that in a society where death-rates are low, the rate of employment high, and social welfare schemes adequate, it is emotional instability and the inability of parents to make effective family relationships which are the outstanding causes of children becoming deprived of a normal home life. This itself is an important conclusion, but it is perhaps even more important to note that the origin of adults being unable to make effective family relationships is not infrequently itself the result of their having been deprived of a normal home life in their own childhood. Thus the investigator discovers a self-perpetuating social circle in which children who are deprived of a normal home life grow up into parents unable to provide a normal home life for their children, thus leading to another generation of adults unable to do the same for theirs.

CHAPTER 9

Prevention of Family Failure

SINCE the basic method of preventing a child from suffering maternal deprivation must be to ensure that he receives nurture within his own family, measures which promote this must be encouraged. On the probable success of such measures the League of Nations Report of 1938 is encouraging. After reviewing the resources available to a skilled caseworker, it concludes that 'in the vast majority of cases, the careful use of such methods and resources ensures a quality of child care sufficient to meet the minimum requirements of the community and there is no need to remove the child from his own home'. Such measures commonly consist of active assistance to the parents, economic, social, and medical.

Three objections are commonly lodged against a society making itself responsible for such action. The first is that of economy. Against this must be considered the immense cost to the community in ill-health, poor work, crime, and the breeding of further deprived children, all of which follow failure to take appropriate measures. The second objection is that providing parents with help undermines their initiative and self-reliance and makes them dependent. This, of course, may follow if the help is given without enlisting the active cooperation of those helped. This, however, need not be. Skilled social workers have learnt to work with their clients, thereby developing their capacity for self-help. Only if the worker permits or encourages dependence by arbitrarily doing things for her clients, without their partaking, need a dependent attitude result. Finally, there is the argument that the State should not intervene in family life. This raises broad issues, but it should be noted that just as children are absolutely dependent on their parents for tenance, so in all but the most primitive communities are their parents, especially their mothers, dependent on a greater society for economic provision. If a community values its children it must cherish their parents.

DIRECT AID TO FAMILIES

Economic Aid

Although the League of Nations Report laid it down that

> it may therefore be regarded as an axiomatic principle of child care that no child should be removed from the care of an otherwise competent parent when the granting of material aid would make such removal unnecessary,

it is clear that this principle has yet to be acted upon in most countries. There are today governments prepared to spend up to £10 a week on the residential care of infants who would tremble to give half this sum to a widow, an unmarried mother, or a grandmother to help her care for the baby at home. Indeed, nothing is more characteristic of both the public and voluntary attitude towards the problem than a willingness to spend large sums of money looking after children away from their homes, combined with a haggling stinginess in giving aid to the home itself. Many examples of this could be given, from the large sums spent to keep a child in hospital compared with the much smaller sums required to treat him at home, to the power of a local authority to spend up to, say, £10 a week providing residence for a child, while being without the power to spend 50*s* or so on bedding to enable him to live at home. Difficulties in regard to differential treatment of families there may be – if Mrs Smith gets blankets, why should not Mrs Jones? – but these difficulties must be solved by methods other than retaining the children in an institution.

In particular, far too little attention has been given to the needs of the home which has lost one parent only through death, illness, or other cause, a condition which is found for about one-quarter of all children in care; clearly every effort must be made to help the other parent care for the children.

Husbandless mothers of children under five, and especially those under three who are still unfitted for nursery school or any form of community life, have the greatest difficulty in most countries in both making a living and caring for the children – activities which are impossible to carry on together when the children are very young. Though direct assistance to the mother is commonly meagre, in many cases public or voluntary funds are spent on the provision of day-nurseries, which in parts of England, for instance, cost nearly £7 per head per week. This is not a fruitful way to spend the money, from the point of view either of health or of industrial production. As regards health, day-nurseries are known to have high rates of infectious illness and are believed to have a bad effect on the children's emotional growth. As regards production, there is little net gain in woman-power, since for every 100 mothers employed fifty workers are necessary to care for the babies and, as every industrialist knows, mothers of young children are unsatisfactory employees and often absent on account of minor illnesses at home. For these reasons day care as a means of helping the husbandless mother should be restricted to children over three who are able to adapt to nursery school. Until a child has reached this age, direct economic assistance should be given to the mother.

In the case of fathers who are left with motherless children, either temporarily while the mother is in hospital, or permanently, the provision of a housekeeper service is much preferable to removing the children. This service, which has been developed in Canada and the U.S.A., is described as follows:

> The time given by the housekeepers varies from two hours a day to resident service, but in several instances the housekeeper has continued with one family for several years. Before house-

keeper service is given, the agency requires that the family shall have one reliable member, usually a father or an older child. . . . It has been said that housekeepers are 'foster-mothers in reverse'. In the case of a foster-mother youth is an asset, but with a housekeeper it is a liability. Another striking difference is that while the foster-mother spends her own money, the housekeeper spends another person's money. . . .

The advantages arising from the housekeeper service have been summarized as follows:

Holds the father's interest and sense of responsibility.

Gives the children more security in their family relationships.

By preserving the home and equipment it avoids the prolonged break-up which generally results from boarding-home placement no matter how devoted the father may be.

Less expensive than boarding care in large families.

More normal relationship and status for a child in the community than if he is in a boarding-home.

Avoids the real tragedy that occurs when a child grows into a boarding-home family and has to be uprooted.

It will be observed that, at least with large families, this method of care is actually cheaper than removing the children.

On grounds of financial economy as well as the child's mental health, then, it is to be hoped that governments and voluntary agencies alike will, before spending more money on the care of children away from their homes, consider whether everything possible has been done financially to assist parents to care for them at home. Spence puts the matter pithily when he remarks: 'Much that passes for social aid to mothers is construed in a way which raises their fears and undermines their confidence. They are relieved of their children when they should be relieved of their chores.'

Socio-medical Aid

Essential though economic aid frequently is, it is often useless unless help of a socio-medical kind is given as well. In many cases there would be no economic problem at all were it not for physical or mental illness, maladjusted character, or conflict in the home.

Although the provision of services for the care of the physical health of parents, especially of mothers of young children, is of the utmost importance, this has now become accepted practice in many Western countries and so need not detain us here. A special service which has not yet received the recognition which it deserves is the provision of rest homes to which mothers may go with their younger children. Such a home has been established near Manchester, since the end of the last war. To this home a mother who is either in physical ill-health or on the verge of a mental breakdown may go for weeks or months for convalescence without the problems of having to arrange for the younger children's care or the anxiety of wondering how they are faring – an anxiety both inevitable and proper for the mother of small children. Moreover, if such a home is run with insight into the emotional problems of mothers and children, much quiet help can be given to the mothers to establish a relationship of security and mutual affection on which, as has been seen, the child's future mental health depends.

Another service which is only as yet in an early stage in most countries is that of marriage counselling. Before effective measures to help married couples who are in difficulties can be devised, there must be a sound understanding of the causes of marriage failure. In several countries there has been considerable emphasis laid on ignorance of the physical side of marriage, but most people with experience now realize that this is only a small – and easily remedied – part of the problem. Far more important are the personalities of the partners. The conclusion of research workers that 'the affectional relationships of childhood condition the love-life of the adult' will be remembered. It is this basic truth which underlies modern methods. An American social worker, writing on the diagnosis and treatment of marriage problems, remarks: 'We see that people who come to us because of marriage difficulty have carried over unresolved childhood problems into the marriage to an extensive degree.' Unless these are clearly recognized and attention given to them, little progress in better adaptation can be effected. In particular, it is necessary for the social worker to be aware both of the strong unconscious drives which lead husbands and wives to create the very problem of which they complain and of the distorted light in which they see the behaviour of their spouse. Not only may husbands and wives provoke a marriage partner to unkind behaviour, but they may genuinely believe that their behaviour is far worse than it really is. The difficulties are thus the difficulties of one or both partners in making satisfactory human relationships.

Although these personality difficulties starting in childhood must be counted as the most frequent and weighty factors in maladjustment in marriage, faults in the social world within which the couple live must not be overlooked. Reference has already been made to the social break-up which characterizes many Western communities of the present day, and this is apt to force husbands and wives to seek within the family the satisfaction of personal and social needs which are by their nature impossible to satisfy there. In these circumstances the family ties are, as it were, carrying an amount of 'current' for which they were not designed, and it is not surprising that what corresponds to 'fusing' is a not infrequent occurrence.

Marriage counselling to be effective must therefore take account both of the whole social setting of the family and also of the internal psychological difficulties of the partners. It must treat not only the symptoms, but the underlying causes of their troubles.

The same considerations apply when there is friction between parents and children, a not infrequent cause of children being removed from home. The particular problem – bedwetting, stealing, aggressiveness, or whatever it may be – is to be thought of as merely the symptom calling attention to a far more complex and often partially hidden situation in which emotional difficulties of the parents usually play a large part. Child-guidance workers clearly recognize this and, despite the name, nowadays give as much time to the treatment of the parents as to that of the children. It is true that at one time child-guidance services themselves were all too frequently the cause of children being removed from home, but the leading clinics in Europe and America no longer look on the removal of the child from home as a wise step. Naturally there are cases where a temporary change may be of value, and others where the child's home is unmendable. However, greater understanding of the working of family relations, combined with greater technical skill in handling them, have gone far to change policy in the direction of mending the home instead of breaking it up. Many seemingly hopeless problems when approached with insight and skill are found to be treatable, since there is in almost all families a strong urge to live together in greater accord, and this provides a powerful motive for favourable change. It is the task of the worker, whether medical or not, to help provide conditions in which this wish can re-assert itself so that, though all may not be perfect, the essential features of a good home are restored. The provision of child-guidance services on a generous scale must therefore be regarded as a first contribution to the maintenance of family life and so to the promotion of mental health. Furthermore, it is now agreed that work of this kind is of particular value in the case of young children and their mothers, since it is in the first few years of life that the pattern of later parent-child relationships is laid down. The troubles of adolescents are often no more than the echoes of conflicts which began in these early years. Difficulties which are insoluble at thirteen may be handled quickly and effectively at three. It is by giving priority to work in these early years that our best hope of prevention lies.

Special educational arrangements for maladjusted children

are also of value. Since 1939, the city of Amsterdam has provided one or two specially staffed day-schools, to which children are referred by its mental health division after thorough psychiatric investigation and diagnosis. There is close contact between teachers and psychiatrists, and special efforts are made to work with the children's parents and to arrange vocational guidance and after-care. More recently the County of London has followed Amsterdam's lead.

In the case of older children – eight years and over – the use of expedients such as boarding-schools may be of value. If the child is maladjusted, it may be useful for him to be away for part of the year from the tensions which produced his difficulties, and if the home is bad in other ways the same is true. The boarding-school has the great advantage of preserving the child's all-important home ties, even if in slightly weakened form, and since it forms a part of the ordinary social pattern of most Western communities today the child who goes to boarding-school will not feel different from other children. Moreover, by relieving the parents of the children for part of the year, it will be made possible for some of them to develop more favourable attitudes towards their children during the remainder.

Finally there is the question of problem families. They may be divided into three groups:

(*a*) Those which, provided economic and medical help can be given, can become once again effective social units;

(*b*) Those which may require some degree of permanent help, but which can respond favourably to it;

(*c*) Those which all ordinary social measures are powerless to assist.

The work required for the first two groups if they are to be put back on their feet again has been well described in the report of Mrs Hubback's Committee – *The Neglected Child and his Family*. Experience has shown that the combination of insight into causes, sympathetic contact, and hard manual work, with medical and financial aid, can save many homes which in other hands would have been morally condemned and broken up. Such help is of particular value where ignorance, poverty, and physical ill-health have been the causes of family failure. Where temperamental instability or psychological illness of the parents is the root cause, such measures commonly fail, and for this reason workers need psychiatric insight if they are to avoid breaking their hearts on cases they cannot help.

There is as yet no agreed plan for tackling families where failure is due to the chronic psychological troubles of the parents. Probably the most sensible and constructive plan is that of placing whole families under supervision and restraint by providing for them special units, each of which can accommodate a small number of problem families and which are the responsibility of trained workers. It is argued that, just as it is regarded as necessary for the sake of their own well-being and the well-being of others to place under supervision individuals who are mentally ill, so is it reasonable to place under supervision those families which are endangering the well-being of their own members and others. A programme of this kind would in almost all countries require legislation, and is now legalized in the Netherlands. It is recognized that this plan 'involves a serious infringement of personal liberty and offers possibilities of abuse', but problem families constitute a very serious and self-perpetuating danger to social progress. Until more effective measures for restoring health to psychologically ill characters can be found, or until long-term measures of mental hygiene have proved successful in preventing their development, this indeed may be the right solution.

LONG-TERM COMMUNITY PROGRAMMES

Economic Developments

The break-up of society and of the greater family in Western industrialized communities sets grave problems.

To discuss how these basic social trends should be reversed or their effects on family life lessened is outside the scope of this book. Nevertheless, a comprehensive policy for the prevention of children becoming 'deprived' cannot afford to ignore them, and in this field the economically less-developed communities may well have much to offer the more-developed ones. One point should be noted – the great economic weakness of the family with children. Beveridge has reported that in England 'a family still remains the greatest single cause of poverty', a còndition which clearly holds true elsewhere in the Western world. This has led in many countries to the provision of family allowances, a vital step in the right direction. Even so, it must be considered whether some specially increased provision should not be made for children under five or three. It has been seen that it is at this age that they are at their most dependent and from a mental health point of view most liable to harm. The mother of young children is far more tied than is the mother of school-age children, for whom part-time work is quite possible. Since the mother of young children is not free, or at least should not be free, to earn, there is a strong argument for increased family allowances for children in these early years.

Socio-medical Developments

An additional reason for adequate and graded family allowances is that poverty, with resultant overwork and under-nourishment, is a powerful cause of parental ill-health, both physical and to a lesser degree mental, and this, as has been seen, is a major cause of children becoming deprived. Even though the foundations of good health can only be laid in a social and economic system which is fair to everyone, personal health services are also essential. Here again parents, and especially mothers of young children, must have priority if family failure is to be avoided.

A special word is appropriate here on the need for long-term programmes of mental hygiene. Hitherto, these have been difficult to plan because of a lack of agreement regarding the origins of mental ill-health. For long it has been known that certain relatively rare conditions are caused by infection and that a few others are inherited. The vast majority of cases, however, have remained a mystery and a source of controversy. This is now changing as evidence accumulates pointing to the child's experience in his family as being of central importance for his healthy emotional development. The outstanding disability of persons suffering from mental illness, it is now realized, is their inability to make and sustain confident, friendly, and cooperative relations with others. The power to do this is as basic to man's nature as are the abilities to digest or to see, and, just as we regard indigestion or failing vision as signs of ill-health, so have we now come to regard the inability to make reasonably cooperative human relations. The growth of this ability, as has been seen, is determined in very high degree by the quality of the child's relation to his parents especially in his early years, hence the desirability of concentrating especially on the treatment and prevention of psychological troubles in childhood.

In practice, this means not only treating children, but the giving of psychiatric help to parents, especially the parents of very young children, who often respond rapidly. Since the need for such help vastly outstrips its supply and an order of priority is unavoidable if rational use is to be made of what exists, pride of place must go to patients who are both of key importance and respond in a quick and lasting way. Those who have worked with the parents, especially the mothers, of young children believe that there is no more fruitful mental hygiene work than this.

In addition, preventive mental hygiene demands early and effective aid to families who have already got into difficulties, including measures to avoid the removal of children from home, and, finally, the best possible provision for children who for any reason cannot remain at home. By such measures it may, in the course of two or three generations, be possible to enable all boys and girls to grow up to become men and women who, given health and economic security, are capable of providing a stable and happy family life for their children. In this way, it may be hoped both to promote mental health and to get rid of very many of the factors which at present cause children to be deprived of maternal care.

The long-term programme of mental hygiene is thus seen to be the psychiatric care of individual families writ large.

This programme for the prevention of family failure, it is recognized, demands great effort. That part of it primarily concerned with social and psychological services, such as marriage counselling, child guidance, and work with the parents of very young children, requires large numbers of skilled workers. Their training and maintenance will take time and money, but is likely in the long run to be a far cheaper and more efficient method of solving the problem of 'homeless children' than the mere provision of foster-homes and institutions.

One question which is likely to be asked is in regard to the position in this programme of professional personnel without psychiatric training – physicians, nurses, social workers, and others. Are they to be excluded from taking part? On the contrary, the answer is simple and clear: only if all these workers are trained can the work be done on the necessary scale. The stage has been reached in preventive medicine in Western countries where disorders springing from infection and malnutrition are, to a large extent, conquered, and where health workers are free to give time and energy to mental health. This is admirable, but, before these workers can be effective, extensive retraining and radical changes in outlook and attitude are necessary. The principles and practice of psychological medicine and preventive mental health cannot be learnt in a few weeks or even a few months any more easily than the principles and practice of physical medicine and preventive physical health can be learnt in this time. Unless the amount of training and change of attitude which are required are clearly recognized and tackled, employment of the non-specialist for this work will prove useless. All those aspiring to work in this field must become thoroughly familiar with the psychology of human relations, alive to unconscious motives, and able to modify them. Such widespread professional training and retraining is today the foremost need, both in mental hygiene and the preservation of the family.

CHAPTER 10

Illegitimacy and Deprivation

ILLEGITIMATE children are not everywhere in Western countries regarded as bringing shame to their mothers, nor themselves made to some extent the victims of this shame. For instance, in some Western communities it is thought wise for a man before marriage to make sure that his future wife can bear him children: in other places it is almost a custom for people to live together as husband and wife without a marriage ceremony: there are also groups of people (usually among the poorer classes) where it is not held against an unmarried girl that she has a child, and her family supports her and her child amongst them.

Official statistics of illegitimacy do not show any difference between these cases of what may be called 'socially accepted' illegitimate children, who are not deprived by their birth of a normal life, and those whose birth outside marriage brings them into grave danger of growing up as deprived children, the 'unaccepted' illegitimates. This book is concerned only with children in this latter situation.

CHARACTER AND HOME BACKGROUND OF PARENTS OF ILLEGITIMATE CHILDREN

Until recently, the fact that some girls become pregnant illicitly was looked upon as something bound to happen and dismissed as just human nature. Apart from moral exhortation, little attention was given to prevention. Studies carried out in America make clear, however, that the girl who has a socially unacceptable illegitimate baby often comes from an unsatisfactory family background and has developed a neurotic character, the illegitimate baby being in the nature of a symptom of her psychological ill-health.

One observer, for instance, carried out a study of 100

unmarried mothers between the ages of eighteen and forty, who, although representing wide variations in intelligence, education, and social and economic backgrounds, were if anything rather above average in intelligence. She found that forty-eight girls had dominating and rejecting mothers and another twenty had dominating and rejecting fathers, and that the girl's relation to the dominant parent 'was a battleground on which a struggle was fought, and the baby was an integral part of that struggle'. No fewer than forty-three of the 100 girls had been brought up in broken homes (a finding confirmed by a Toronto study which gives a figure of thirty broken homes in the histories of fifty-seven unmarried mothers, and a further ten with quarrelling parents). All the girls studied in this investigation had grown up to have

fundamental problems in their relationships with other people. Some of them could not carry on even superficial contacts successfully; others did well with casual acquaintances and friends, but were unable to enter into close or intimate relationship with anyone. . . . The problems followed them into their work and few of them were able to use more than a small part of their native intelligence and ability. . . . All these girls, unhappy and driven by unconscious needs, had blindly sought a way out of their emotional dilemma by having an out-of-wedlock child. It is not strange that one finds among them almost no girl who has genuinely cared for or been happy with the father of her baby.

Practically none of these girls was promiscuous in her sexual relations and only one-quarter of the group had had more than a fleeting relationship with the father of the child. In all of them there appeared a strong unconscious desire to become pregnant, motivated sometimes by the need for a love-object which they had never had and sometimes by the desire to use the shame of an illegitimate baby as a weapon against their dominating parents. It was noteworthy that a large group insisted in a rigid and unreasoning way on their mother looking after the baby, despite her objections. Running side by side with the need to use the baby as a weapon against the parents was the need to use it as a weapon against themselves – a deep, ingrained desire to punish themselves, sometimes very powerful and obstinate, the result of profound feelings of guilt.

Though it is impossible to know how typical these findings are, it is the opinion of many social workers with psychiatric knowledge and experience of this problem that with many girls becoming an unmarried mother is neurotic and not just accidental. In other cases the girls are chronically maladjusted or defective. For instance, of ninety-three unmarried mothers whose children were in the care of Dr Barnardo's Homes, twenty-five are described as moral defectives, and were no doubt promiscuous, a further ten were dull and backward, mentally defective, or insane. No particulars are given regarding the others, though some, no doubt, were similar in character to those described above.

The character of the unmarried father is rarely studied and not much is known of him. It is the opinion of experienced social workers that many are unstable and that they often promise marriage irresponsibly. Compared to the unmarried mother, they are more often promiscuous and get several girls into trouble within a short time. The psychology of habitually promiscuous men has been studied in connexion with the prevention of venereal disease. One psychiatrist, after studying 200 soldiers suffering from this disease and a comparable group numbering 861, concluded:

> The all-round picture which emerges is that venereal disease patients are often emotionally, sexually, and socially immature, whereas physically and intellectually they may have reached full maturity.

Among factors which make for promiscuity, this worker lists the need for affection, situations which arouse anxiety, and situations which arouse resentment. He does not think an overstrong sex instinct is of great importance.

In seeking to understand the origins of these unstable, immature characters, whose anti-social behaviour brings so much misery in its train, one is led back, as in the case of many unmarried mothers, to their childhoods and their relationships with their own parents. In a study of 255 promiscuous men it was discovered that 60 per cent came from homes which had been broken by death, separation, or divorce, the average age of the child when the home broke up being six years.

> Among the patients whose homes had been broken, it was not unusual for the patient to have been placed in boarding schools, foster-homes, institutions, or in the homes of relatives. A number of the patients had had a series of such placements. Some patients had had no care by either parent from birth or shortly thereafter. Some of those had been born out of wedlock. In other instances one or both parents had remarried and the patients were reared in homes with stepfathers or stepmothers. The patients reported difficulties in adjusting to successive changes in the family pattern. Inconsistencies in training and discipline were frequently the result of constant shifting from the care of one parent to that of another. . . . Conflicts were most pronounced in the cases where the family life had been unstable and the patient had been entrusted to the care of first one person and then another.

This picture is confirmed by other evidence.

Preliminary studies such as these go far to show that, in a Western community, it is emotionally disturbed men and women who produce illegitimate children of a socially unacceptable kind. Moreover, they give further prominence to the social process already emphasized as being of the greatest consequence for the production of children who will grow up deprived of maternal care – the process whereby one generation of deprived children provides the parents of the next generation of deprived children.

CARE OF ILLEGITIMATES

There are two ways of approaching the problem of preventing the illegitimate child becoming in need of care away from home – to prevent his being conceived and to make sensible plans for his care if he is. How to bring down the birth-rate of socially unacceptable illegitimates is a matter for long-term measures of mental hygiene. Meanwhile it seems likely that for many years to come Western communities will have to face the problem of how best to care for such children. Though it is evident that in this, as in all problems, the most effective measures are possible only if there is real knowledge and understanding, the absence of studies on how illegitimates may best be cared for is conspicuous.

In several countries of Europe, e.g. the Netherlands, Sweden, and the United Kingdom, policy has been strongly in favour of the unmarried mother keeping her child. For instance, in a circular issued by the British Ministry of Health, the duties of a social worker in helping the unmarried mother are stated as, first 'whenever possible to persuade the girl to make known her circumstances to her parents and, if the home is likely to be a satisfactory one, to persuade the grandparents to make a home there for the little one', to continue by considering alternatives such as residential employment, day nurseries, foster-homes, or residential nurseries, and only 'in special cases, e.g. where the mother is very young, or is the wife of a man not the father of the child, to give advice about legal adoption'. Yet when one inquires in these countries for studies of how the illegitimate child who is not adopted actually fares little is available. Reports such as that of the Medical Officer of Health for Willesden are far from reassuring, however. In a very disturbing account of the hazardous and ever-changing lives of foster-children in the borough in 1939 he writes:

> The majority of foster-children are illegitimate. Their mothers are frequently in employment and may work up to a month before confinement. During this last month when they are not employed they must keep themselves and make some provision for the child. They are generally confined in hospital. At the end of ten days or a fortnight they are discharged. They have no money left. They

have nowhere to go. They are handicapped by the child. It is important that they get work at once. What often happens seems to be that such a mother finds some woman who, perhaps out of kindness or perhaps in hope of money later on, takes the child whilst the mother searches for work. The child may be well cared for or not, but in any case the mother probably in the circumstances does not inquire too closely. She is glad to get anybody to take the child. If she gets work and pays the woman it may be that the child stays on for a time, but if the payments are small and irregular the child may be passed from one woman to another, finding no stability in life at all.

One London society concerned with the care of unmarried mothers, reporting on the placement of over 1,000 babies in the period 1949–50, shows that 22 per cent were placed with foster-parents or in a residential nursery soon after birth. Only 17 per cent were adopted. The bulk of the remainder were living with their unmarried mothers. That many of these will sooner or later also find their way into foster-homes or nurseries is indicated by another London society which, stating that it is its policy in all suitable cases to encourage unmarried mothers to keep the custody of their children and to give the mothers, when necessary, financial and other assistance to make it possible, proceeds: 'It has to be faced however that lack of accommodation makes it increasingly difficult for an unmarried mother to have her baby with her continually from its birth, and during some considerable part of its childhood it is more than likely to be fostered or placed in a residential nursery.'

The paucity of satisfactory figures for countries of Western Europe is a measure of their neglect of this problem, while such information as is available makes it clear that in some countries at least a large fraction of illegitimates, perhaps more than half, under the present haphazard arrangements grow up suffering from some degree of maternal deprivation and into characters likely to produce more of their kind. Though people are apt to express very strong views as to what course is in the best interests of unmarried mothers, the public shows as little concern about knowing what actually happens to them as in the case of their children, since there seem to be no studies of this in any Western European country.

But the picture in Canada and the U.S.A. is rather different. There have been a few studies of what has actually happened to illegitimates who have not been adopted. In 1943 a study was published of the history and adjustment of illegitimate children aged fourteen and fifteen years who had remained with their mothers or relatives in Toronto. Of the ninety-two children studied (forty-nine boys, forty-three girls) only twenty-five had remained with the same family group since birth, though a further nineteen had been accompanied by their mothers through a variety of changing circumstances. The remaining forty-eight (52 per cent) had changed their mother-figures – usually two, three, or more times. The study goes further, however, in that it demonstrates first that a large proportion of these children (47 per cent) are showing signs of maladjustment, and secondly that this is related to their experiences. In particular, it is found that the earlier the child is settled the better – hardly a surprising conclusion. In twenty-one cases (seventeen boys, four girls) their maladjustment took the form of delinquency, mostly stealing and truancy. One girl of fifteen had already run away and become pregnant – another example of the vicious circle of the deprived reproducing themselves. How many of the other twenty delinquents – nearly one-quarter of the whole group – will grow up to produce illegitimate or deprived children?

The report states that with few exceptions the homes from which the delinquents came were unstable and unhappy. 'Children were taken out of homes where they were happy and thought they belonged into homes where they were not wanted. Others have been rejected practically since birth by the people with whom they lived.' Here is more evidence, if it is still needed, that deprivation causes maladjustment and delinquency.

The Toronto inquiry reveals a sorry state of affairs, which its authors believe is due to the policy pursued by the societies advising these unmarried mothers at the time of the children's births – that the unmarried mother should look after her own baby. It was clear that this rather rigid policy had over-influenced many of the mothers, some of whom having cared for their babies whilst they were very small found it impossible to give them up later, even when they learned that the future offered little opportunity for satisfactory living for themselves, and little chance of normal growth for their children. Others had quickly rebelled against the societies' rulings and had got rid of their children as best they could. In other cases again the mother's parents had been forced, urged, or encouraged to provide homes, although the relationship between the mother and her parents had for long been unhappy, with the result that the baby became the cause of yet further friction. Naturally, there were cases where the arrangement of the mother or her parents looking after the baby had worked well, but this seems to have occurred only when the mother was stable, had good relations with her parents, and was fond of the baby and his father – not a very frequent set of circumstances.

A little earlier, in New York, a worker had studied thirty mothers who had committed their illegitimate babies to an institution whilst waiting to make a final decision, and had come to a similar conclusion. Of the thirty, only eight were finally taken home by their mothers, four were adopted and, after a lapse of three years, fifteen remained in the institution or in foster-homes. But not only were half of these mothers still unable to come to a long-term decision after three years, but it is probable that the outcome could have been accurately predicted from the time of the baby's birth. Only if at least four of the following conditions are present is the mother likely to take the baby home: that she is a stable personality, takes a sensible attitude towards her problem, is loving and accepting of the child, really cared for the supposed father, and has a family which does not insist on the child being disposed of. Such conditions are likely to be present in only a minority of cases.

Of the group of children whose mothers neither relinquish nor take responsibility for them, a very experienced social worker has written:

> The child continues in an institution or foster-home, or more likely a series of foster-homes, a tragic example of nobody's child. The mother visits occasionally. She may bring him presents. Rarely she pays a little for his board. When asked about plans for him she always reiterates that some day she will take him, but that some day never seems to come. By the time the Society is convinced of the need for an enforced surrender, the child has probably grown beyond the age when he can easily be placed for adoption.

In a booklet published by the Children's Bureau of the U.S. Department of Labor, this illustration is given:

> One such child at ten years of age is a disturbed, bewildered boy with many behaviour problems. He has lived in twenty foster-homes. At the time of his birth his mother was a docile, receptive girl who agreed with the philosophy of the maternity home that she should keep her baby. Her parents refused to allow her to live at home if she kept him. She went to work in a store, paid the child's board regularly, and visited him in the foster-home every two weeks. Gradually, however, her payments stopped. Twice she attempted suicide. Either the original plan was an unsuitable one for both her and the child, or the mother was not given enough case-work assistance in carrying out the plan.

As a result of histories such as these, progressive policy in the U.S.A. in regard to illegitimates has changed abruptly and far more adoptions are being arranged. Social workers now conceive it to be their duty to help the unmarried mother face the real situation before her, which so often is that of an immature girl, on bad terms with her family, with no financial security, having to undertake with little or no help the care of an infant for whom she has mixed feelings, over a period of many years. If this is in fact the real situation and it is put before her in a sympathetic way by someone whom she has learned to trust, many girls recognize that it is in the interest of neither themselves nor the baby to attempt to care for him, and are prepared to release him for adoption. American social workers have become self-critical of their previous inclination to avoid responsibility for making a long-term plan and for unwittingly helping the unmarried mother herself to evade it. For this is in fact what voluntary societies and public agencies are doing when they receive illegitimate children into care without insisting that the mothers either make practical long-term plans to provide care themselves, or else permit others to do so – by arranging adoption.

Unfortunately, instead of considering simply what is best for the child and what is best for the mother, workers of all kinds have too often been influenced by punishing or sentimental attitudes towards the erring mother. At one time the punitive attitude took the form of removing the baby from his mother as a punishment for her sins. More recently this punitive attitude has led in the opposite direction and has insisted that she should take the responsibility of caring for what she has so irresponsibly produced. In a similar way, sentimentalism can lead to either conclusion. Only by getting away from these irrational attitudes and preparing to study the problem afresh is a practical set of working principles likely to be adopted. It is urgently necessary in many countries to make studies of what in fact happens to the illegitimate children of today – how many achieve a satisfactory home life with their mothers or immediate relatives, how many eke out their existence in foster-homes or institutions, and how many are adopted, and what is the outcome. Furthermore, it is necessary to study the development of the unmarried mother and to devise means of helping her avoid such tangles in the future and to achieve a more satisfactory way of life. It may perhaps be that, in some cases, encouraging her to take the responsibility for her baby will help her to become a more responsible citizen, but to act on the assumption that this is always the case is not only to be unpractical, but to be socially irresponsible ourselves. For it is a very serious thing to condemn a child to be parked in an endless succession of foster-homes or to be brought up in an institution when there are long waiting lists of suitable parents wishing to adopt children.

Hitherto most nations have preferred to forget the existence of illegitimate children or, in so far as they have aided them, it has been too little and too late. If a community is to remove this source of deprived children, it will have to be more practical in its handling of the problem, both by providing economic and psychological assistance to the unmarried mother to enable her to care for her child and by providing skilled services to arrange for the adoption of those children who cannot be so cared for.

CHAPTER II

Substitute Families

I. ADOPTION

'THE central paradox of work for deprived children is that there are thousands of childless homes crying out for children and hundreds of Homes filled with children in need of family life.' This situation, graphically described in the Annual Report of the Children's Officer of an English borough, occurs in many Western countries. Yet very little serious study has been given to the problems of adoption, and it is only gradually becoming recognized as a process requiring scientific understanding and professional skill. Too often the baby's future is the concern only of a well-meaning amateur or of a doctor or other medical worker concerned only with physical health. Once again scientific studies of the subject are conspicuous by their scarcity.

The process of adoption concerns three sets of people – the mother, the baby (almost always illegitimate), and the prospective adopters. There is skilled work to be done with each. First, help must be given to the mother to enable her to reach a sound decision; this requires skill in making a relationship of confidence with her, in understanding her personality and her social situation, and in helping her face unpalatable facts in a constructive way. Secondly, there must be an ability to judge how the baby is likely to turn out – no easy task and one about which there are many ungrounded beliefs. Finally, there must be an ability to predict how a couple will care for children, often in the absence of any direct demonstration of their capacities, and to help them in the early adjustments. These are formidable tasks. Furthermore, they must be discharged reasonably quickly since all with experience are agreed that the baby should be adopted as early in his life as possible.

The evidence given earlier in this book points unmistakably to its being in the interests of the adopted baby's mental health for him to be adopted soon after birth. No other arrangement permits continuity of mothering and most other arrangements fail even to ensure that he gets any. If the baby remains with his mother, it is not unlikely that she will neglect and reject him; if he is parked temporarily in a nursery or group foster-home his development will often suffer in some degree. Nothing is more tragic than good adoptive parents who accept for adoption a child whose early experiences have led to disturbed personality development which nothing they can now do will put right. Very early adoption is thus clearly in the interests also of the adoptive parents. Moreover, the nearer to birth that they have had him the more will they feel the baby is their own and the easier will it be for them to identify themselves with his personality. Favourable relationships will then have the best chance to develop.

The arguments *against* very early adoption are three in number:

(*a*) It requires what might be a hurried decision by the mother.

(*b*) The baby cannot be breast-fed.

(*c*) There is less opportunity to judge the baby's probable development.

Of these the first argument is the most weighty. It is clearly of the greatest importance not only that the right decision should be reached by the mother, but that it should be reached by her in a way which leaves her convinced that she has decided wisely. This may take time, though no good comes from prolonging the period of indecision indefinitely. If the mother has sought care reasonably early it should be possible for the experienced case-worker to help her reach a wise decision either before the baby is born or soon after, since most of the factors which matter (e.g. stability of personality, attitude towards the problem, and attitude towards the father) will be evident in her life before the birth of the baby. If all of these are adverse the baby's birth will not change them, and the likelihood is small of the mother making a success of looking after the child. More knowledge, skill, and sense on the part of case-workers could undoubtedly lead to wise and emotionally satisfactory decisions being reached fairly early in a large proportion of cases.

Moreover, it is in the mother's interest to make the decision to keep or part with her baby early rather than late. Unless it is reasonably clear that she will be able to care for the child, it is no kindness to permit her to become attached to him; parting is then all the more heart-breaking. Some unmarried mothers decide, after reflection, that they would prefer not to see their babies, a decision which should be respected. Rigid policies that all unmarried mothers must care for their babies for three or six months and must breast-feed them can have no place in a service designed to help illegitimate babies and their unmarried mothers to live happy and useful lives.

It is, of course, only when a baby is likely to be breast-fed that the interruption of breast-feeding is an argument against early adoption, since if the mother is unwilling to feed the baby or if he is to be deposited in a nursery or foster-home the question does not arise. If early adoption does in fact mean depriving a baby of breast-feeding, it is, of course, a matter for concern. Even so, to reach the correct decision regarding the best age for the child to be adopted requires the weighing of one set of medical disadvantages against another and only far more research than has been done into the bad effects of each can allow a really sound decision. Meanwhile, it is unwise to assume that breast-feeding and later adoption is better for the baby's future welfare than early adoption and affectionate artificial feeding.

The third argument against early adoption – that there is less opportunity to judge the baby's likely development – is commonly used by psychologists, but is the weakest of the three. It rests on the assumption that the various tests of development available in the first year of life can really foretell the child's later mental development. An exhaustive inquiry has shown that this is not so. Tests of a baby's development during his first eighteen months give no trustworthy evidence of school-age capacity. Not only is this so, but, as has been seen, there is a very serious danger that keeping a baby in a nursery awaiting adoption in the belief that in a few more months an accurate prediction can be made will itself check development, which is then taken as evidence that the baby is naturally backward. Hence there develops the paradoxical situation in which misguided caution in arranging adoption creates a baby which at first appears and ultimately becomes unfitted for it.

Probably the best guide to the child's likely intelligence is the intelligence of the parents, though for many reasons this can be no more than a very rough guide and adoptive parents like natural parents must be prepared to take a normal risk.

It will be seen, therefore, that the arguments against early adoption are far less strong than they appear at first sight. On psychiatric and social grounds adoption in the first two months should become the rule, though some flexibility will always be necessary to permit mothers to work their way to a satisfactory decision. If during the waiting period the baby is not cared for by his mother it is preferable for him to be cared for in a temporary foster-home rather than in an institutional nursery.

To dub a baby unfit for adoption is usually to condemn him to a deprived childhood and an unhappy life. Few are qualified to reach this decision and the grounds on which it is commonly reached today in Western countries are more often well-meaning than well-informed. For instance, many adoption agencies place an absolute bar on the children of incestuous relationships, however good the stock. Naïve theories of heredity may also lead to a child being blackballed for such reasons as having a brother or sister mentally defective or a parent suffering from mental illness. In the days when it was the accepted psychiatric view that all mental illness was hereditary this may have been a reasonable policy. Now that this is no longer so, it is unreasonable, except in those cases where the amount of mental defect or illness in the family is clearly much above the average. It has already been remarked that mental tests have no predictive value in the first eighteen months of life, so that some backwardness, even in the absence of deprivation, need not be taken seriously unless it is very marked. Finally, the widespread assumption that children with certain physical handicaps are unfit for adoption is ungrounded, as has been shown in an interesting paper entitled *The Unadoptable Baby Achieves Adoption.*

Three principles thus emerge from discussion of a baby's suitability for adoption:

(*a*) That judgement of the child's inherited powers requires the opinion of a person with training in human inheritance and that in no case should a decision against a child be reached without the opinion of a competent person;

(*b*) That psychologists should be thoroughly familiar with the predictive value of their tests and with the effects of deprivation, illness, and other circumstances on test performance;

(*c*) That even if the child's state, or the probabilities about his future, are not wholly favourable, an attempt should still be made to see whether there may be adoptive parents who, after being given full knowledge of the facts, are prepared to accept him with understanding.

The third area in which knowledge and skill is required is in estimating would-be adoptive parents and in helping those who are suitable to adjust happily to the intense emotional experience of adopting a baby. Here there is no place for the amateur, whose only standards can be outward signs of respectability, or the worker trained only in physical hygiene with her standards of income, cleanliness, and cubic feet of air space. These standards have led to irrelevant and fancy demands. The baby's mental health will depend on the emotional relationships he will have the opportunity to develop; and their prediction requires good knowledge of the psychology of personality and skill in interviewing. The most important thing is to estimate the real motives behind the mother's desire to adopt a baby (it being almost always the mother rather than the father who is the architect of the plan). These motives are often not what they appear to be and their true nature may be largely concealed from the woman herself. It is not to be held against foster-parents that they are searching for love, or more love, or a different kind of love: that in itself tells something about them. But what is important is the *kind* of demands they make, such as laying down exact particulars of age, intelligence, the standing of the real parents, their nationality and temperament, and sometimes sticking to these demands even when shown that they are unreasonable. A woman may insist on a girl of a particular colouring, or a man may cling to his determination to adopt a boy who will be all that he would have liked to be. These inflexible and egoistic requests are in contrast to those of adopters who can consider a reasonable range of children.

Those adopting these rigid attitudes are doing so for reasons connected with their own emotional conflicts deriving from their own childhoods. In such a case the child is needed not for himself, but as the solution of a private difficulty in a parent and, as might be expected, more often than not provides no such solution. The woman who has always felt unloved and who seeks love and companionship from the baby will not wish him to grow up, make friends, and marry. The woman who seeks a little girl who will achieve all that she has failed to achieve is likely sooner or later to be disappointed and to turn against her. Many other unsatisfactory motives may underlie the demand for a child. In the same way satisfactory motives may masquerade under exteriors which seem unpromising. The woman with a gauche brusque manner or the easy-going, untidy and not too clean couple may none the less have warm hearts and prove loving and effective parents. If their motives are right much else can be overlooked.

How is the social worker to discover their true motives? Partly by inquiring how it was that they first thought of adopting a baby and partly by learning more about them as people, especially their capacity to make easy and loving relationships with others. In estimating these, three principal opportunities offer – the way they speak about other people, especially their relatives; the way they treat each other; and the way they treat the social worker. It is particularly important to know what their marriage has been like. Yet this is precisely the area most commonly evaded by the interviewer who, unless thoroughly trained, feels, and is, quite incapable of making inquiries which are both useful and yet not embarassing.

The relationship between proposed adoptive-parents and worker is also valuable for finding out what sort of people they are:

> Families who resented the worker's interest in their intimate lives, or felt that their references, position, or deep need for parenthood entitled them to a child with no questions asked, often were reflecting underlying problems bearing an important relation to parental capacity. Often, too, the families who easily established a relationship with a worker, who recognized the agency's need to choose good parents for children and admitted to human qualms, problems and imperfections, were revealing deep assets for parenthood.

The capacity to face difficulties in a courageous way and to consider soberly how best to meet them is indispensable in adoptive parents, for 'the ability to take some risks is essential for adoptive parenthood' as it is for natural parenthood.

> The question is not whether we can match their need surely in

a child's infancy: for we plainly cannot. The question is rather what they would do with disappointment; and whether they could still function as loving parents, satisfied in their parenthood. There is no such thing, unfortunately, as a 'guaranteed adoption'; no children an agency can safely mark 'Certified'. It is vital, therefore, that parents be able to accept a child whether or not he can measure up to their hopes and wishes for him.

Flexibility and the capacity to face the truth are clearly desirable if the parents are to tell the child of his adoption, a practice which all are agreed is essential, since sooner or later the truth will become known. So long as the parents can themselves admit the truth and do not have to cling for personal reasons to the fantasy of having produced the child themselves, there need be no great difficulty in bringing the child up from earliest years in the knowledge that he has been adopted. Complications will arise only if the natural and adoptive parents know each other. Reputable workers usually preserve absolute secrecy on this matter, and there seems no doubt that this is essential if the adoption is not to be endangered.

The intense emotional experience of a parent who adopts a baby is often overlooked. An excitement, urgency, and deep feeling often show in the adoptive mother's attitude. To her it means not only taking possession for better or for worse of a human life, and with it all that the possession of a baby means to a woman, but it may mean also the final acceptance both for her and for her husband of the painful fact that they will never have a baby of their own. These are difficult and conflicting emotions which, if not worked through, may linger to mar the parents' feelings for the baby. Once again insight based on knowledge and skill based on training are required. Similarly, knowledge and skill are necessary in the social worker when she has to tell parents that they are not suitable. Naturally, she will try to put it to them in the least painful form to avoid distressing them more than necessary, but her principal aim must be to help them see the truth for themselves, for unless she can do this the prospective parents will not only feel disgruntled, but will persist in their search for a baby to adopt.

Not much is heard of the black market in babies – the process whereby would-be adopters who have been refused by reputable societies succeed, sometimes by the payment of large sums to third parties, in securing a baby for themselves. In most countries at present this can be done by people whom all would agree are quite unfit to care for a child. It is a social and legal problem which one day will require attention, but it would be foolish to tackle so thorny a problem before the recognized machinery for adoption is in the hands of qualified people who can be relied upon to make sound judgement of prospective parents. This will take time.

It has already been remarked that prediction of how the baby will develop is an exceedingly difficult task, and for this reason the matching of baby and parents is more easily desired than achieved. Moreover, so long as there are queues of parents waiting for a trickle of babies, the parents may feel thankful to get any child. Race, and to some extent colouring, can be matched fairly easily, and by matching social class the securing of comparable intelligence is the more likely. Until predictions of other characteristics can be made more sure, time spent on looking into them is largely window-dressing.

Finally, it may be asked what is the proportion of adoptions which are successful. This, of course, is a relative question, the results depending largely on the skill of the society arranging them. What one needs to know is the proportion of successes when adoption is carried out by skilled workers. No adequate study seems to have been made, though one investigation in New York into fifty adopted children after they had reached the age of four showed only six cases of parents whose attitude was unfavourable. But these figures are not enough upon which to make a final judgement. If we are really to understand them we must take into account such matters as the age at which the children were adopted, and the standards of success used by the investigators. They should also be compared with similar studies of children cared for by their own parents. Judged by the latter standard, so far as is known, the proportion of successful to unsuccessful adoptions does not seem unsatisfactory. This agrees with the experience of the child-guidance clinics, who do not have an undue proportion of adopted children brought to them. From these meagre facts it may be supposed that in skilled hands adoption can give a child nearly as good a chance of a happy home life as that of the child brought up in his own home. Even so, the information we have is deplorably inadequate and, if these problems are to be taken seriously, will need to be greatly increased.

CHAPTER 12

Substitute Families

II. FOSTER-HOMES

It has been insisted throughout this book that the right place for a child is in his own home, or, if he is illegitimate, perhaps in an adoptive home, and because of this measures for preventing family failure (or for arranging permanent and early adoption) have been explored at some length. These must always be used to the full before other substitute homes are considered. It is recognized, however, that there are bound to be a few children who will need emergency or more prolonged care outside their homes, and attention must now be turned to the best methods for its provision. First, emergency care will be considered.

EMERGENCY CARE

There are many unforseeable events such as death or sudden illness of the mother which require immediate action for the care of the children: in others, for instance when the mother is going to have a baby or an operation, the need for temporary care is forseeable. Such cases represent a very high proportion of all those needing care. In England, the Curtis Report quotes them as being about 60 per cent of all children requiring care, while at the home through which pass all children over twelve months coming into care in Stockholm, 70 per cent stay for one to eight weeks only. Since the circumstances of such children should be well known and the future arrangements either already settled or about to be settled, they are to be sharply distinguished from cases where family discord, delinquency, or neglect set difficult questions and the future is obscure. The building of large reception homes to which children of *all* kinds coming into care must go for observation and sorting is not desirable. The main arguments against such an arrangement are:

(*a*) That two entirely different problems are confused;

(*b*) That there are better alternatives for short-stay children;

(*c*) That when children are likely to be long-stay cases, it is usually best to observe them and decide what they need by seeing them as out-patients;

(*d*) That the size of the institution required to deal with both short-stay cases and observation cases together becomes unwieldy.

There is, however, a place for the small reception centre restricted to taking children over five years of age who unexpectedly require immediate shelter. Their stay, however, should be thought of in terms of a few days only, and should not be dragged out over weeks or months.

There are various alternatives for handling these temporary emergency cases, and different methods need to be employed for different age-groups. For children over six or seven years, especially adolescents, group care in small centres, described in the next chapter, is satisfactory. Children of these ages can fend for themselves for a short time in such an atmosphere, and are better not put under the strain of having to develop a relationship with members of an unknown foster-home for a brief time. This consideration, however, does not apply to infants and young children, who, all the evidence shows, are unable to adapt to group conditions. For them it may be recommended that the plan adopted by a number of agencies on both sides of the Atlantic, should become general – the keeping of a register of foster-mothers who are qualified and willing to take a couple of infants or toddlers for brief periods and who are paid a retaining fee, so that vacancies are always available at short notice. Work of this kind might solve the economic problems of many widows with young children.

It may well be, however, that a better solution for all age-groups lies in getting the help of relatives and neighbours. It has already been remarked that governments and voluntary bodies are slow to support children in their own families and relatively quick to spend money on institutional care. A similar lack of wisdom in spending money is shown when children are taken into care without every effort being made to get relatives to act as substitute parents. It may be that they live far away or that they are not well off financially. But the cost of railway fares for even some hundreds of miles, together with the payment of maintenance costs, is as nothing to the cost of providing full care for a child. In this connexion, the provision in English law whereby a relative may be officially registered as a foster-mother and paid as such is a most valuable one. Naturally, discretion must be used before employing relatives. If they are complete strangers to the child their value is thereby greatly lessened, while if one of a married couple is opposed to it the child becomes the centre of friction in the new family. Nevertheless, close relatives known to the children are far more likely to have a strong sense of obligation to them than are strangers, and the value of familiarity to the child is boundless.

For the same reason, neighbours may be especially valuable as temporary foster-parents. Not only does the child remain with familiar faces in a familiar place, but the neighbours themselves, because they know the children and their parents, are likely to give the children a warmer welcome and greater security than would strangers. It is thus most important that any child-care agency should do its utmost to encourage a sense of neighbourly pride in looking after such children for a time. Parents should be helped to realize that it is in the children's interest to remain with friends, and that it is in their own interest to share in an arrangement whereby all householders give aid to each other in a family emergency. In encouraging such a spirit, the agencies themselves must use common sense about standards of cleanliness, sanitation, and comfort. Sometimes it is difficult in a given neighbourhood to find houses which meet the usual standards in this respect, but since it is probable that in this case the child himself comes from a similar home, no great harm will be done if he spends a few weeks in another. If, for purposes of temporary care, it were agreed that so long as the foster-home is equal to or better than the child's own home in respect of such matters no further questions need be asked, many more temporary homes could be found and many more children would be cared for in emergency within sight of their own homes.

Moreover, neighbourhood care of short-stay children would get rid of one of the greatest dangers attending the removal of children from their homes – that of the children being left in temporary care for an indefinite period. To those unfamiliar with the problem this may seem odd, but the reality of the danger is known to social workers both in America and Europe. Going over the cases of children in institutions and foster-care has on many occasions revealed that a majority of them have lingered on for months and years after the emergency has passed and could have returned home long since. Such inaction appears to spring both from the parents' side and from that of the society. Some less responsible parents are content to let things slide and, if the case is neglected long enough, come to adapt their way of life to the absence of the children, making conditions increasingly difficult for the child's return. Other parents, of the more simple-minded kind, are impressed by the generous material conditions in which the children are placed and modestly feel they are better off where they are. This attitude, it must be admitted, is sometimes encouraged by societies, whose pride in the services they render may blind them to the vital need of the child for a continuous intimate relationship which it is so difficult to provide outside his own home circle. This blindness, if coupled with a lack of skilled case-workers, can very easily lead to the agency itself making worse the very problem it is meant to solve. In the words of an English children's officer: 'A long-stay case is generally a short-stay case which has been mishandled.'

The need for the earliest possible return home of all children placed away is now clearly recognized by all good agencies, and to enable this to be done it is agreed that a large part of the work of a child-care agency, whether responsible for children in foster-homes or institutions, will lie with their parents. This is particularly important when the child comes from a home where there is family discord and neglect, and where the parents' unwillingness to carry out their responsibilities is too often aided by well-meaning but unskilled methods.

SOME PRINCIPLES OF CHILD CARE

In the past, and far too often even now, there has been a reluctance on the part of agencies to recognize the following three principles:

(*a*) A clean cut cannot be made between a child and his home.

(*b*) Neither foster-homes nor institutions can provide children with the security and affection which they need; for the child they always have a makeshift quality.

(*c*) Day-to-day arrangements create insecurity in the child and dissatisfaction in the foster-mother; sensible long-term plans are essential from the beginning if the child is not to suffer.

An exceedingly common mistake has been the belief that removing a child from his home will lead him to forget it and to start afresh – and the worse the home, it has been supposed, the more easily will he do so. This false belief has led to the practice of forbidding parents and children to see each other in the belief that the children will then settle better. These assumptions flout all that is known about young children and fly in the face of good evidence. Two studies may be quoted. In the survey of children evacuated to Cambridge during the Second World War, it was found that parents' visits were not harmful, but actually helpful to the child's settling down in a foster-home. Even before this, two workers in the U.S.A. had carried out a systematic study in which they compared the degree of security shown in the behaviour of children who were permitted some contacts with their previous homes (either their own or a foster-home) with that of those who were not. The observations showed that the children who had been completely separated from all touch with their former homes were on the whole more insecure and difficult than those who were allowed some contact with their previous surroundings.

These studies confirm what is already known about children, namely, that they are not slates from which the past can be rubbed by a duster or sponge, but human beings who carry their previous experiences with them and whose behaviour in the present is profoundly affected by what has gone before. It confirms, too, the deep emotional significance of the parent–child tie which, though it can be greatly distorted, is not to be got rid of by mere physical separation. Finally, it confirms the knowledge that it is always easier for a human being to adapt himself well to something of which he has direct experience than to something which is absent and imagined.

It is the realization that the child in a foster-home (or institution) is living in two worlds – the foster-home (or institution) and his own home – which has led to the new outlook on child care. No longer does the social worker imagine that it is possible to find a home which a child will regard as a complete substitute for his own. However good the foster-mother or house-mother, the child will regard her as a more or less poor makeshift for his own mother, to be left as soon as possible. Only if a child is placed before the age of about two is he likely to feel otherwise. And, because the social worker knows how the child will feel, she is able to help the foster-mother to understand the temporary nature of the situation and to adapt to it; for to encourage a foster-mother to believe that she will get all the satisfactions of a real mother is merely to raise hopes that will be dashed. Moreover, the social worker, realizing the significance which a child's own parents have for him, will realize the necessity, if his future is to be assured, of helping them too. Before, therefore, considering the long-debated issue of how to care for a child away from home, it is necessary to consider some of the essential work which must be done with parents if placement anywhere outside his natural home is to be a constructive step in a child's life and lead to his future happiness, and not to a long-drawn-out period of uncertainty and indecision during which his misery and sense of insecurity lead him either to shut himself in a shell or to become actively troublesome.

CASE-WORK WITH PARENTS

Perhaps no child-care practice has been more common or more damaging than that of agencies accepting children from 'bad' parents on a 'temporary' basis without plan for the future. This system of indefinite care and uncertain responsibility discourages a relationship between parents and their children and ignores a child's need to be deeply loved and to have deeply rooted ties in a family. Clearly no system is better calculated to discourage the half-hearted parent or to weaken a feeble sense of responsibility than to permit an indefinite postponement of decision while relieving the parents of immediate care. This reminds us of the hand-to-mouth methods so common in the management of illegitimates.

Instead of unwittingly aiding irresponsibility for the child's future, agencies, whether voluntary or governmental, must make it their first task to help the parents recognize the origins of the problem and make a sound plan for the future. This means that the agency gives its help conditionally – conditionally on the parents maintaining responsibility for the child's future to the utmost of their capacity. As in all case-work service, the process must begin at the first moment of contact, when the parent's need makes him most ready to face unwelcome truths.

The parent is held to the need to examine the nature of the neglect, to determine what he can do about it, to explore whether that will help meet the child's needs, and to recognize how the agency stands ready to help him achieve for the child the needed care and security. . . . [He] must be helped to know the limitations as well as the advantages of boarding care as the case worker knows them.

Here, perhaps, is the crux of the matter – 'as the case-worker knows them'. So long as case-workers do not know these limitations, but live, as some do, in the sentimental glamour of saving neglected children from wicked parents, they will act impetuously in relieving parents of their responsibilities and, by their actions, convey to the parents the belief that the child is far better off in the care of others. Only if the case-worker is mature enough and trained enough to respect even bad parents and to balance the less-evident long-term considerations against the manifest and perhaps urgent short-term ones, will she help the parents themselves and do a good turn to the child.

Naturally, by the time parents come to the point of handing over their children, or authorities deem the children to be in need of care, the home situation is likely to be very bad. Immediate and practical decisions about the long-term future may consequently be impossible. But if the social worker, by her first handling of the case, makes it apparent that her help depends on a long-term solution being found within a reasonable time, and that this can only be one of two alternatives – the parents taking care of the child at home again or releasing him for permanent placement – and that in her view the parents themselves are vital people in the child's life, and so must share in the planning of his future, all but the most maladjusted parents will respond.

Only if the parents are treated in this way, moreover, are

they likely to play a useful part in any foster-care arrangements which the agency may make. So long as they are left out of planning, they will either throw up all responsibility and disappear from the child's life or else interfere in an haphazard and unpredictable way. Such interference is extremely common and constantly complained of; but it is inevitable when agencies leave the parents out of the planning and leave them also to face alone the puzzling emotional problems which have so often led to placement – and the additional problems to which it may give rise; in particular, a sense of guilt at having rejected their children and fear of being blamed by other people as inadequate parents.

The records of all agencies are full of evidence of the difficulties created for children in long-term care by their parents' inability to permit them to settle in a foster-home and to feel part of it. Parents feel jealous of the foster-parents and make trouble, or they resent them and refuse to visit. The children are left in a turmoil of conflicting loyalties. In one child-guidance clinic by far the most difficult cases of disturbed foster-children were those whose parents remained in a conflict of feeling about placement and 'carried on an active but irregular connexion with the child'. Of fifty disturbed foster-children attending the clinic in Philadelphia, seventeen fell into this class; they showed a great variety of problems – truancy, stealing, lying, open sex behaviour, bedwetting, speech defects, physical disorders, nervousness, severe temper tantrums. In only four was successful treatment possible.

Admittedly such parents are very difficult to manage, and it is because of this that case-workers of the highest skill are required when the children are first brought into care, which, as already emphasized, is by far the most hopeful moment for influencing them. And it will be readily observed that the skill required is skill in handling contradictory and unconscious motives. Only if such skill is available is one of these neurotic parents likely to work well with the agency and make the child's placement a fruitful period instead of a harmful one. This is a principal reason why child-care agencies are appointing psychiatric consultants to aid them.

CASE-WORK WITH FOSTER-PARENTS

We have emphasized the importance of case-work with parents because, despite its being the key to success, it is still too often neglected. Case-work with foster-parents and with foster-children is also vital. Apart from the obvious importance of selecting suitable foster-parents and the need to know the foster-parents and the child so that they may be sensibly matched, there is the need to prepare foster-parents unsentimentally for the behaviour which the selected child is likely to show. This is too often evaded because of the pressure to find foster-parents and the reluctance to discourage any who may seem appropriate. Yet, unless the case-worker takes the foster-parents into his confidence about the children and their parents, he can hardly be surprised if they are frequently disappointed later and ask for the child's removal – the well-known bugbear of those who arrange foster-home care. They will not behave responsibly towards the agency if the agency fails to behave responsibly towards them.

A special part of these preplacement discussions will be concerned with explaining the child's relation to his own parents, the need for them to visit and how they are likely to behave, and the fact that the foster-parents must not expect the child to behave as though he were their own. The nature of the probable long-term plan will be broached, the foster-parents' comments invited, and their share in planning the future welcomed.

This emphasis on regarding foster-parents as partners in a difficult professional task is in marked contrast to the traditional relationship in which the child-care worker treats the foster-mother rather as she would a patient. This new professional partnership, moreover, uncovers afresh the running sore of the problem of payments for foster-care. Here the tradition has been to pay a bare subsistence allowance, based usually on the cost of living of some few years previous. There has been much resistance to the idea of a wage being paid to a foster-parent, and the argument still continues to be used that to do so creates the danger for a child that foster-care may be given for money instead of for love. This hoary argument, which obtains no support from professional social workers, is clung to by governmental agencies for reasons which it is difficult to dissociate from their desire for economy. To 'fear that paying the foster-mother will affect the natural affection and concern she has for children' is as absurd as 'believing that one's doctor or dentist is less interested in his patient if he may expect to be paid for his services'.

Social workers are unanimous that caring for a foster-child is a real job to be paid for, and point out that in days gone by the children used to make their stay economically worth while through work. Moreover, it must be recalled that the letting value of an extra bedroom and the earning possibilities for a housewife through part-time work are both profitable alternatives to taking a foster-child. In this refusal to pay foster-parents a proper wage, coupled with the substantial sums which voluntary and governmental agencies pay for care in institutions, are seen once again the contrasting degrees of generosity with which they support respectively family and institutional care.

In developing the semi-professional status of foster-parents, it is recommended that they be treated as external members of staff of the agency. It is confidently believed that if this were done, and if they were paid for their services, more responsible foster-parents with better educational background would be forthcoming. Until measures of this kind are taken, national administrations will continue to bemoan the difficulty in finding foster-parents – the universal complaint today.

CASE-WORK WITH CHILDREN IN PLACEMENT

So far work with parents and foster-parents has been discussed; but it is time to consider the child, who, as previously remarked, is too often treated as an inanimate object to be posted from one place to another, in the belief that he will not even carry with him the postmarks of the places to which he has previously been sent. It has been already shown that links with previous homes are best maintained and that the idea of 'clean breaks' is illusory. Much other evidence shows that the more actively a child can be helped to share in the plans being made for him and the more he is helped to understand what they are, for how long they will last, and the reasons for them, the more likely is the placement to be a success.

It is particularly difficult to make successful placements in the case of children removed from neglectful parents by order of court. In such cases there is usually no opportunity to prepare the child for placement, and it is difficult for him to understand why he is being removed from home. He may be resentful and is certainly not ready or willing to accept substitute parents. These facts merit more attention than they have received from those responsible for making court orders.

Because of the great importance of a child's attitude for the success or failure of his placement, social workers are now giving much time and attention to discussing with him both the present position and future plans. This may be done in various ways. One method is to be particularly recommended – that of the social worker holding joint interviews with parents and child, in which the whole situation is thoroughly gone into and a common plan reached. This method of reducing family tensions by a joint interview, stormy though it often is, is a first-hand demonstration to both parties that the professional worker is neutral and is not arranging things privately with one party behind the other's back, a suspicion which is very likely to arise after individual interviews. Another useful point is for a child to be given the chance to know something of his new foster-parents before placement is made, just as the foster-parents have been given the chance to know something about the child. This information may be given both in conversation and by personal visits, which may be several in number, and include, perhaps, a week-end or two when the child stays with the foster-parents and each gets to know the other. This introductory process is not to be neglected in even young children. Right down to the age of two a period of mutual introduction is necessary and valuable, for, as is known, nothing alarms a young child more than being left with strangers.

Furthermore, social workers and psychiatrists emphasize how a child needs to be helped in his new relationship if he is not to spoil it.

> For the child, separation and placement are fraught with emotions of fear, apprehension, anger, despair, and guilt which may be expressed in as many ways as there are defences. . . . Unless the child can accept the necessity for placement, he cannot use his foster home experience. In his denial of his situation, his energies, either in reality or fantasy, are bent on getting back to his parents.

The trained case-worker with psychological insight into these complicated and conflicting emotions can go far to help a child to put his feelings into words and work through them, so that he really accepts the situation. Left to himself, he may well remain in the confused emotional conflict, which results in an incident such as that of the child who proclaimed to the worker on Tuesday that he never wished to see his mother again – his foster-family was his home; and on Wednesday ran away to his mother!

Not only must a social worker do her best to inform a child of what is going to happen and the reasons for it, but she must not forget that one explanation alone may not be enough, nor that the truth which she thinks she has fully explained one day may be overwhelmed the next by misconstructions based either on phantasies or on remarks by parents and foster-parents which have been misleading. The experienced social worker will, therefore, never assume that one explanation is enough – the matter needs to be talked over often, and all the misconceptions dealt with sympathetically. Not infrequently, for instance, children will assume that the home has broken up because of their bad behaviour or that they have been sent away as a punishment – ideas which, if left to embed themselves, can make it impossible for the children to settle in even the best foster-homes and cause great difficulties in later life. In handling these perplexities of children, a social worker needs much skill, for children are well known to be chary of confessing their true feelings and very good at camouflage. An apparent desire to go home may cover a fear of returning, and an external calm hide a broken heart. Once again psychological skill of a high order is required if the work is to be well done.

The extent to which children grieve over separation from their parents has been little appreciated – indeed, it is only in the past ten years or so that grief in early childhood has been given the central position in medicine which it now holds. For long it has been the tradition that the less children are encouraged to express their distress at death or separation the better – they would then get over it more quickly. This view is not supported by modern knowledge. 'If the sorrow of death falls upon a family,' writes Sir James Spence, 'it should not be hidden from the children. They should share in the weeping naturally and completely, and emerge from it enriched but unharmed.' In helping the children experience their grief, the grown-ups have a vital role to play, whether it be death or absence which is being mourned. As regards absence, Mrs Burlingham and Miss Freud, drawing on their residential nursery experience, write:

Mothers are commonly advised not to visit their children during the first fortnight after separation. It is the common opinion that the pain of separation will then pass more quickly and cause less disturbance. In reality it is the very quickness of the child's break with the mother which contains all the dangers of abnormal consequences. Long drawn-out separation may bring more visible pain, but it is less harmful because it gives the child time to accompany the events with his reactions, to work through his own feelings over and over again, to find outward expressions for his state of mind, i.e. to react slowly. Reactions which do not even reach the child's consciousness can do incalculable harm to his normality.

The tears renewed at each visit are always distressing to grown-ups, who constantly feel that a child is best sheltered from these upsetting events. Only insightful understanding of the part they play in his future emotional development will enable the grown-ups to realize that they are worth while, an understanding made easier by recalling the value to adults of being able to weep over a bereavement.

THE CHILD OF PSYCHOPATHIC PARENTS

There is one particular type of child with whom special work is required – the child of parents who are maladjusted and delinquent and actively bad influences. In handling them the case-worker must first get rid of the notion that because of 'bad heredity' these children are likely to turn out less favourably than those without such a supposed handicap. Reference has been made on an earlier page to the follow-up in adult life of children placed away from home and note taken that heredity, so far as it could be determined, had no effect on success or failure: the results may now be given more fully. There were 492 children about whose families something was known. These were divided into three groups, according to whether the parents were both fairly satisfactory characters (good), one satisfactory and one unsatisfactory (mixed), or both unsatisfactory (bad). By unsatisfactory is meant parents who were feeble-minded, alcoholic, immoral, shiftless, etc. Though to a small extent those of bad parentage turned out less socially capable in later life, the difference was only very slight. This result fits in with the too little known principle of human inheritance – that the external characteristics of parents are but a poor guide to the inherited endowment of their children.

In working with children of apparently bad stock results almost as successful as in the case of those from good stock may therefore be confidently expected. This is encouraging. The task, however, remains of discussing with them, or of weaning them away from, parents who are psychologically unfit and actively bad influences. Once again the tradition has been one of evasion and secrecy, and once again it is now known that success demands facing the facts and truth. It might, for instance, be asked, how can the fact that his parents are in gaol, or his mother a prostitute, be discussed with a child? The problem becomes less difficult if the worker is not afraid of these topics herself and recalls that the child, having lived with such proceedings all his life, may know more about them than she herself does, although he may well be unable to adapt himself to the clear conflict between his parents' standards and those he meets elsewhere. Only when the worker can discuss the parents without judgement, spoken or implied, can she help him to consider the problem and understand its meaning; and she needs to realize that one of the principal reasons for his conflict is his determination to see his parents as good figures and his corresponding reluctance to recognize other people's standards as better. This is so important that we must go into it rather more closely.

Throughout this book it has been emphasized that the young child is wholly dependent for his welfare and for life itself on the care bestowed on him by grown-ups, and that, since his parents normally fill this role, it is his parents who are all-important to him. No great war leader saving his country from defeat is more revered than a father or mother, and it is a universal characteristic of children to defend their parents' power for good if this is assailed. This was forcibly shown by a group of schoolchildren who were shown a film, designed to teach road-safety, in which the father made a traffic error and was corrected by his son, the hero of the story. All the children, in spite of having identified themselves with the boy-hero who had many feats to his credit, strongly objected to the father of the hero making a dangerous traffic mistake. The father had to be a good and capable father who would not endanger his son's life.

It is this spirit of loyalty and this need to see the parents as good which demands respect and understanding if we are to help a child gradually to grow away from parents who are unmistakably bad influences. If criticizing a parent may lead to a passionate defence and a child's removal to a romantic idealization of his parent, what, it may be asked, is to be our policy? This has been well described in a paper, *The Hidden Parent*, in which is discussed the secret influence on a child of a parent who, though apparently out of the child's life, is none the less recalled and admired. The author gives two case-histories of children from really bad homes who had been with foster-parents from an early age; though they had appeared to settle down and progress well, both in adolescence had developed all their parents' faults. In neither case had anyone dared to talk to them about their parents. Of a girl whose mother was a prostitute we read:

She should have been not only allowed but even encouraged to ask questions, and to speak of her mother. Someone should have acknowledged to her that of course she loved her. Almost everyone loves his mother; in fact there's something wrong if you do not, not if you do. Once then the child learned that no one would condemn her for wanting to love her mother, and that she no longer had to defend her against the criticisms of people, she could be encouraged to talk of her resentment and anger over the fact that her mother had let her down, had failed to be the kind of mother that she should have been. Through such steps, it would not have been necessary for the child to have repressed her love and hatred to such an extent that they operated like a fifth column within, undermining all the good toward which our efforts were directed. Talking would have released some of the tensions associated with these two feelings, and left the child freer to pattern her life after that of the foster mother's.

This is in fact the experience of those workers who have used this method with skill. At first the child can admit of no defects in his parent. Then he begins to sway between defence and criticism, with outbursts, perhaps, of very bitter feeling. Later again he is able to take a more unprejudiced view – to see her as someone with shortcomings as well as virtues, even to understand her as an unhappy person who has made a failure of life. This is often the easier for him if the parent's unsatisfactory behaviour can be related to the difficult childhood she may have had, since the child has first-hand experience of the way in which difficult home situations can create emotional problems for people. By working through violent and contradictory feelings to a more sober and reasonable view, a child ceases to be the victim of irrational ties to an unsatisfactory parent and is able to make an adjustment to the brutal truth – that his parent is no good to him and that he must seek affection and security elsewhere.

It must be admitted that helping a child in this way is not easy and requires of a social worker not only understanding, but emotional toleration of many feelings which are personally upsetting – angry feelings for good parents or foster-parents, admiration for bad ones. Yet, difficult and upsetting though these things may be, they are the forces that will mar the child's life, the time-fuses that will lead to explosion if they are not removed.

This discussion has led time and again to recognition of the need for honesty, for frankness in facing disagreeable truths, and for calling spades spades. Parents need to be encouraged to realize that because of the nature of children's feelings for them they have tremendous power over their happiness, a power which they cannot get rid of, try as they will. Foster-parents are to be helped to recognize the ties which bind children to neglectful parents and to tolerate the cool ingratitude with which the children respond to their kindness. Children are to be encouraged to express both affection for bad parents and anger for their neglectfulness, emotions which seem either unreasonable, unnatural, or to contradict each other. Moreover, all three parties, however irresponsible, however ill-educated, however young, are to be encouraged to take part in the planning of the future on a level of equality with the mature, educated, and benevolent social worker. All this may seem topsy-turvy to those still working in the spirit of the nineteenth century, yet these are the great lessons which psychological knowledge has to teach. To Freud is due the credit for discovering not only that human beings nurse in their hearts many fearful and horrifying emotions and are prone to wish outrageous things, but that they have also tremendous capacities for good and, above all, that human nature can master the most distressing facts and the most appalling calamities if it is helped squarely to face the truth.

In discussing foster-placement the emphasis has deliberately been placed on the psychological methods which should be employed. These ways of working with parents, with foster-parents, and with the children themselves may seem time-consuming and even fancy, but the issues at stake, the child's future health, happiness, and usefulness as a citizen – and the manifestly unsatisfactory results of more slapdash methods – must be remembered. It must be recognized, too, that failure is as often due to lack of skill in planting the child in a new home as it is to the unsuitability of one to the other – the usual reason given. Moreover, it is because the subject has been so neglected that it has been considered essential to discuss the methods of placement before the methods of selection. To the latter brief attention must now be given.

MATCHING OF CHILD AND FOSTER-HOME

Probably the most important single factor to be borne in mind when selecting temporary foster-homes is that of the motives of the prospective foster-parents; this was emphasized also in selecting homes for permanent adoption. Naturally, when temporary placement is the plan and the child is to keep in touch with his own parents who will be encouraged to visit him, the motives will be different from those found in adoptive parents, but the social worker has to be equally clear about their nature and will find the same methods of inquiry applicable. Childless couples are not usually very well suited to be temporary foster-parents, as they are likely to become too possessive, and success is more common with parents whose children are beginning to grow up. On the other hand, foster-parents over sixty are less likely to be successful than younger ones. But perhaps more important than these standards is the need for selecting foster-parents who are able to work in close association with a social worker and who are not too proud to ask for and to accept help.

Apart, however, from the question of whether a given foster-home should be used at all is the important matter of matching child and foster-parents. It has been noted that a great deal of billeting difficulty during the war would have been avoided if the human relationships involved in placement had been given as much thought as the administrative ones.

Among situations which are favourable in foster-homes are:

(*a*) The presence of other children in the home, especially brothers and sisters of the foster-child. It is found particularly important for girls over twelve to be placed with other children.

(*b*) A difference of four years or more (in either direction) between a foster-child and the foster-parents' own child of the same sex.

(*c*) The placing of a child of the opposite sex to, but of the same age as, the foster-child works well.

(*d*) Nervous anxious children are best placed in quiet conventional types of home, while the active aggressive children are best in free and easy homes with companions, though wherever placed it is this type which gives rise to most difficulty.

Situations to be avoided wherever possible include:

(*a*) The older the child the less suitable is he for a foster-home. This is especially true of children over thirteen years.

(*b*) Young children (under ten years) are not well suited to elderly foster-parents (over forty-five years).

(*c*) A foster-child of the same age and sex as a child of the foster-parents gives rise to friction. Such a child is thought of too much for his uses as a playmate and too little for himself. Moreover, situations of jealousy and rivalry are apt more often to arise than where age or sex are different.

(*d*) Large differences in standards of living and social class between foster-family and the real family have sometimes been found to prove a strain for the child and to make for resentment or jealousy in the real parent.

(*e*) It is a great mistake to put seriously maladjusted children in foster-homes before the children are well on the way to recovery. It has been frequently found that the placing of such cases leads to failure, especially amongst the children whose anxiety shows itself in rudeness and aggressiveness. The 'shut-in' type of child succeeds better.

These limited conclusions are given both as guidance for practice and as an illustration of what can be confirmed or discovered by careful scientific surveys.

One observer in the Netherlands says of the foster-children he studied:

It appeared that even with the best selection and preparation, both of the child and of the parents, 20 per cent of the children had difficulties of adjustment in the new family. These difficulties were noted specially with children who in their earliest years had not had contact with their own family or a strong relationship with their mother.

These, of course, are the severely deprived children discussed in Part I of this book.

The layman sometimes has great difficulty in accepting the opinions of mental health workers that a very large fraction of children coming into care are emotionally maladjusted. He complains that psychiatrists and their colleagues see disturbances where none exists, and have protested that in any case provided such children are given care and kindness time will heal their troubles. It cannot be too strongly emphasized that those with training in mental health do not share this optimism. The truth is that in peace time a child needing prolonged placement is as likely as not to be a maladjusted child, and that, unless this maladjustment is recognized and plans for his placement made appropriately, the tragic procession from one foster-home where he fails to settle to another is likely to follow. Foster-mothers cannot for long give loving care to a child who fails utterly to respond.

Though it is universally agreed that foster-home care is, in general, greatly to be preferred to group care, the unsuitability of certain children for foster-homes makes it necessary to provide group care for them. The following chapter is, therefore, devoted to the principles which should underlie its provision.

CHAPTER 13

Group Care

THE controversy over the merits of foster-homes and of institutional care can now be regarded as settled. Though there is no one who advocates the care of children in large groups – indeed, all advise most strongly against it, for reasons which will be evident to the reader of the first part of this book – there is widespread agreement regarding the value of small specialized institutions. These have been found to serve best many of the following types of children:

(*a*) The seriously maladjusted child who is unable until improved to make an effective relation to foster-parents. The organization of treatment centres for such children is discussed in the next chapter.

(*b*) Adolescents who are no longer dependent on daily personal care and who, partly because they can so easily maintain an emotional relation with their own parents, even in their absence, do not readily accept strangers in a parental role. An exception to this is the adolescent who is leaving school and starting work, and who may, as part of the process of earning a living and growing up, settle down easily in a foster-home.

(*c*) Children over the age of six or seven who are in need of short-term care only.

(*d*) Children whose parents feel threatened by the relationship between their child and foster-parents and who may need an interval before deciding whether to take their children back home or to release them to live in a foster-family.

(*e*) Large groups of brothers and sisters which might otherwise have to be split up among several foster-homes. An important exception to this principle of keeping family groups together is in the case of infants and toddlers, who cannot in such circumstances obtain the essential individual care they need unless the home they are in is very small.

So many wise books and reports have appeared of recent years on the principles which should be followed in organizing institutions for children that little discussion is called for here. All are agreed that institutions should be small – certainly not greater than the 100 children suggested by the Curtis Report – in order both to avoid the rules and regulations which cannot be avoided in large establishments, and to permit the children to attend the local schools and in others ways to take part in the life of the local community without flooding it. All are agreed, too, on the need for the children to be split up into small 'family' groups of varying ages and both sexes, each in the charge of a house-mother, and preferably also of a house-father, an arrangement which not only encourages some of the emotional atmosphere of a family to develop, but also permits of brothers and sisters remaining together to give each other comfort and support. (Nothing is more tragic and destructive of mental health than a system that divides children by age and sex and thus splits up families of brothers and sisters.) 'Family' groups must be kept small; the Curtis Report recommends eight as ideal and twelve as the maximum. Informal and individual discipline based on personal relations instead of impersonal rules is possible only in these circumstances. It must be recognized, however, that even in such relatively favourable circumstances it remains very difficult to avoid some of the undesirable characteristics of an institution – uniform regulations between cottages, personal friction between members of the staff, and some measure of divorce from the rough and tumble of ordinary social life. Flexibility and allowance for personal differences of character are apt to be lost and the children have little opportunity for taking part in creating the conditions in which they live. This deadening of initiative and removal of responsibility is an evil influence in institutional life.

To overcome it, the scattered cottage home is widely advocated, an arrangement which can also be described as a large professional foster-home. Thus, local authorities in England are adapting for this purpose pairs of ordinary semi-detached houses on new housing estates and placing a married couple in charge of each. The husband goes out to work, the wife housekeeps, the children mix with the local children and differences from the lives of ordinary children are kept as small as possible. For its success this system needs foster-parents of good quality, able to bear considerable responsibility, and these, it must be emphasized, cannot be obtained cheaply. Where foster-parents have not these qualities, and perhaps usually where unmarried foster-mothers are employed, the group of cottage-homes may be better, since it provides more support. Whichever system is adopted, certain central services can be provided with a saving of labour and cost, though it must be remembered that in providing these there is a danger of taking too much personal choice out of the hands of the foster-mothers. For instance, if stores are provided centrally there is no need for shopping or the choosing of food, both of which are very important parts of domestic life. A compromise must be made between the economy and the monotony which come when much is organized from the centre and the variety coupled with increased work which are the result of more being left to the foster-parents.

Among other things, a house-parent must not attempt to own the children and must encourage parents to visit and so promote parent–child relations. That house-mothers require training and that their work should be put on a professional basis is now recognized. It is important, too, that their role in relation to other professional workers – social workers, psychiatrists, and others – should be made clear, so that good team-work is possible. Regular discussions regarding the children in their care should form a recognized part of their duties, and they should be encouraged to discuss their problems with psychiatric consultants, who must of course also be trained for this work.

The medical care of the children must in future include care of their mental health, and in this connexion further experiments are needed in the use of observations of changes in height and weight, which may prove to be a valuable method of discovering emotional disturbances in children who seem to be well settled and happy. These hidden disturbances, often of grave psychiatric significance, are common in institutions. All with mental health training emphasize the deceptiveness of the children's behaviour, especially when it consists of passive obedience to the authorities. Children in institutions tend to develop a double standard of morals: an external obedience to regulations and an internal standard which may be thoroughly delinquent and which only declares itself later. An example of this comes from Chicago: when children who had long been in an institution, and who there seemed nice and polite, were distributed to foster-homes, it was apparent that they were afraid of close personal contacts and seemed to prefer living in an emotional vacuum. They avoided making decisions, resented suggestions of independence, and made excessive material demands. It is important to recognize that these unfavourable traits emerged only when they left the institution – while they were in it all had seemed well, at least to the superficial eye. There is a similar report on an examination of a group of six- to eight-year-old children, none of whom was considered in any way abnormal by those who managed the institution in which they lived. Though the first impression of them was rather favourable – 'they seemed to have an unusual amount of group spirit' – further examination showed them to lack all adaptability. In a way typical of institution children, they were hungry for toys and demanded to hold the grown-ups' hands. In spite of good intelligence, all conception of time, space, and person was lacking. Here, in fact, were affectionless and sick characters masquerading as normal children; as might be expected, they had been brought up in the institution from an early age. This leads back to the central theme of this book – the care of infants and young children.

RESIDENTIAL NURSERIES

Unfortunately the idea sometimes persists that institutional conditions do not matter in the case of babies and toddlers. It is therefore vital to note that there is no support among those with mental health training for this complacent view. All are strongly opposed to it. Clear statements to this effect are to be found in the writings of all those psychologists and psychiatrists who have undertaken research on the problem. As long ago as 1938 the matter was publicly discussed in the League of Nations Report, which tells of the difficulties which institutions experience in caring for 'infants and very young children (who) appear to thrive better and to develop more quickly and vigorously under individual attention and in an atmosphere of family affection'. It is therefore distressing that some years later, when much more scientific information was available, the Curtis Committee advocated 'residential nurseries for all children up to twelve months and for older infants not over two and a half years and not yet boarded out or placed in a family group'. Clearly this must be regarded as a most serious shortcoming in an otherwise progressive report. It is much to be hoped that this particular recommendation is not followed either in Britain or elsewhere, and it is satisfactory to find that the official policy of the United States Children's Bureau is against residential nurseries and in favour of the care of infants and young children in foster-homes.

It cannot be too strongly emphasized that with the best will in the world a residential nursery cannot provide a satisfactory emotional environment for infants and young children. This is not merely an idea which comes from theories, it is the considered opinion of prominent practical workers in many different countries. For instance, in England Mrs Burlingham and Miss Freud reached it as a result of their experience in running a residential nursery during the war. At first they were hopeful of solving the problem, but as time went on they became increasingly aware of the evil effects of maternal deprivation and of the difficulties of providing substitute care in an institutional setting. In the end they concluded that so many helpers were necessary if their infants and young children were to receive the continuous care of a permanent mother-substitute, which their observations showed to be essential, that it would be better to arrange for each helper to take a couple of children home with her and close the nursery. In the U.S.A. and in the Netherlands experienced workers have also found from personal experience that young children thrive much better under individual care than in nurseries.

The reasons why the group care of infants and young children must always be unsatisfactory is not only the impossibility of providing mothering of an adequate and continuous kind, but also the great difficulty of giving a number of toddlers the opportunity for taking an active part in the daily life of the group which is of the utmost importance for their social and intellectual development. Even in a family with only two or three under-fives and a full-time mother caring for them, it is very exhausting for her to permit the children to 'help' her in the daily tasks of feeding, washing, dressing, dusting, and so on. When there are many it is almost inevitable for the children to be excluded from these activities and to be expected to be obedient and quiet. The institution child cannot take part in the daily round of family life and has no continuous social intercourse with grown-ups. The frustration to which this can give rise is shown by the alternative responses of apathy and violent aggression, the extent of which is not easily believed by those without experience of what can go on in such circumstances.

Unfortunately, national policy in many countries still

tolerates residential nurseries, the ill-effects of which it is sometimes attempted to lessen by regulations which, so long as nurseries remain in existence, may perhaps be better than nothing. To avoid the worst effects, the nursery, helpers and children, must be split up into small stable family groups, each preferably with its own pair of rooms – for sleeping, and for eating and playing. Ample toys must be provided with plenty of opportunity for the children to keep some for their very own. Medical inspection, especially against the very common infectious diseases, is now taken for granted, but it is to be hoped that in future this inspection will include also care for mental health. It should become accepted practice that children in nurseries should have psychological tests at regular and frequent intervals, much as they now have their temperatures taken. If such tests were in use at least there would be knowledge of any psychological damage which was being done instead of, as at present, those responsible remaining in ignorance of the matter and able blandly to affirm that the children are 'perfectly all right'. The result of such regular testing may also be expected to hasten the day when residential nurseries, except for the most temporary emergency case, will be commonly recognized as contrary to sound policies of mental hygiene.

STUDY HOMES OR OBSERVATION CENTRES

All concerned with the care of children away from their own homes have been impressed by the necessity of a thorough knowledge of a child if the right provision is to be made for him. There is much less agreement, however, as to how this knowledge is best obtained.

There are two principal schools of thought: either that there should be residential observation centres, or, on the other hand, that the work is best done on an out-patient basis. The first solution was at one time accepted in two European countries with national policies for the care of homeless children – Sweden and the United Kingdom. The Child Welfare Board of Stockholm laid down that all children needing foster-care must pass through their large centre, built in 1938, which also houses short-stay children. Observation and diagnosis were carried out during a stay of some weeks or months with the assistance of a full-time child psychiatrist and a number of kindergarten teachers trained in play methods. In 1949 the United Kingdom also officially adopted this policy, partly as a result of Swedish experience.

There are many workers with mental health training in both Sweden and the United Kingdom who believe that a policy whereby *all* such children have to pass through an observation centre is greatly mistaken, and this view is sustained by many with experience of the matter in the U.S.A. Those who take this opposite view believe, first, that it is better for a child not to suffer an inevitably unsettling experience, and, secondly, that diagnosis can be made as well or better by out-patient methods.

The first question must be: Can accurate diagnoses be made under out-patient conditions? If they can, the expense and effort of setting up observation centres is clearly unjustified – and many child psychiatrists and social workers with experience believe that they can. A child psychiatrist with extensive experience of the problem in Boston, writes: 'Ordinary study cases are best studied in out-patient clinics against the background of their own homes.' A child caseworker in Cleveland, after remarking on the artificiality of separating study from treatment and the unsettling effect of study homes, comes to the same conclusion. A leading agency in Chicago recently closed its observation centre as a result of experience: they had found that the most useful information was contained in the social history taken by a skilled social worker, to which could be added a psychological and physical examination carried out in an out-patient clinic. Information, obtained at first hand by the social worker, on the child's behaviour in his home and on his relation to herself during a brief outing made for the purpose, they believe, is more reliable for foretelling how the child will turn out than that obtained in the conditions of a reception centre.

One of the difficulties in reaching a diagnosis is, of course, that of deciding whether difficult behaviour or neurotic symptoms are reactions to present bad circumstances or are already embedded in the child's personality. In tackling this problem it is possible, in addition to examining the child himself, to proceed along two different lines: (*a*) that of taking a detailed history of his behaviour and symptoms in all known situations, present and past (at home, in school, with relatives, with foster-parents, etc), and of his personal experiences in relation to grown-ups, especially parents; and (*b*) that of removing him from his home and placing him in an entirely new environment. Those with experience regard the former line as the more reliable, since it taps a much wider variety of information. Moreover, the second method is deceptively simple and can be very seriously misleading, since it is well known that children are apt to behave in an uncharacteristic way in strange surroundings. This is particularly true of children under five, as every nursery-school teacher knows. Behaviour in this age-group depends on factors such as space, personality of grown-up, and the number, age, and sex of other children: 'a child may be extremely sympathetic one day in one group and very aggressive the next day with a different combination of children.' Moreover, children are bound to be affected by the situation in which they find themselves at the time, or more precisely which they *believe* they are in at the time, which may be very different and very difficult to discover.

The inexperienced observer is apt to cling with extraordinary tenacity to the view that what he happened to see of the child is of tremendous significance. Tommy was seen to hit another child three times – therefore he is an aggressive boy. Mary spent hours sitting by herself in a corner – therefore she is a solitary child. Such conclusions may, of course, be true, but it is known that they are sufficiently often false to call into question the whole value of observations made in these artificial surroundings.

There is also a danger that a stay in a reception or observation centre may come to be regarded by administrators as a quick and easy solution of family difficulties, and that children will consequently be unnecessarily removed from their homes. As such, it may become a bad substitute for thorough social investigation and family case-work. This is, no doubt, a grave danger. Indeed, it is probably only because of a lack of adequate social and child-guidance services that a belief in the necessity for widespread observation centres ever developed.

Further, the danger that a stay in an observation centre will have a bad effect on a child and his parents must be noted. Psychiatrists in Stockholm have been concerned to find that some children passing through the city's observation centre show signs of 'hospitalism' on reaching their foster-homes. The pioneer centre in Kent, England, reports that 'removing a child from its home, even for a short period of investigation, can have an adverse effect upon his relationship with his parents, especially when the removal comes after a family crisis which may have made him feel hostile to them or rejected by them'. Children under five or six, of course, are particularly likely to be harmed by these experiences. The report rightly emphasizes that 'any effective attempt to reassure the child must be based on an understanding of his private terrors and regrets, which he may hardly have recognized clearly himself'. It underlines the need for 'as early and close a contact as possible between the child and the social worker or official who will be dealing with him after he leaves the Centre'. In all this, needless to say, absolute frankness with the child regarding his position and his future is essential. With all these precautions, however, it is exceedingly difficult to make the stay a healing and constructive one and not just one more period of unsettlement and anxiety. Neither should the unfortunate effect on parents be forgotten – family ties and a sense of responsibility are not encouraged by the children's removal.

Though the conclusion may be drawn that for the great majority of children observation centres are unnecessary, and for children under five a danger, there will always be a small minority for whom temporary care for investigation is needed. These are particularly children who have no home whatever or about whom it is impossible to obtain a reasonably adequate history, conditions which are apt to be found together. In the U.S.A., the practice has grown up of placing these children in temporary foster-homes specially selected for the purpose. In such conditions there is greater opportunity to reach a sound judgement as to the child's capacity to make relationships with parent-substitutes and, therefore, to forecast development. Some foster-parents, especially those who have had children of their own, are interested in this special work, for which they must, of course, be properly paid.

Children who are clearly very disturbed emotionally are best placed at once in a treatment centre for child psychiatric cases, more of which are needed in all countries. Children deemed by the courts to be in need of care and protection are usually best observed while remaining at home. Another week or two in unsatisfactory conditions is unlikely to make a difference to their future (unless of course the parents are likely to be vindictive), and a smooth and planned transfer to other conditions will make for successful placement. The impetuosity and impatience of the outraged official must be resisted.

It is probably only for the older boy or girl who is a delinquent and a danger both to himself and to others that observation centres are really needed; these are usually called remand homes, and their consideration lies outside the scope of this report.

*

To sum up, then, it may be said that group residential care is always to be avoided for those under about six years, that it is suitable for short-stay children between six and twelve, and for both short-stay and some long-stay adolescents. It is also indispensable for many maladjusted children with whose care the next chapter deals.

CHAPTER 14

Care of Maladjusted and Sick Children

CARE OF MALADJUSTED CHILDREN

THERE are three groups of children away from their homes who need special psychiatric care:

(*a*) Those who are suffering from psychiatric disability and who are removed from their homes by legal, medical, or social agents, for reasons either of treatment or to prevent their harming other people. Such disabilities may or may not be the result of bad home conditions.

(*b*) Those, such as were described in the last chapter, whose psychiatric disabilities have been caused by their experiences in institutions and foster-homes.

(*c*) Those whose disabilities have resulted from the unhappy experiences in their own homes which were the cause of their coming into care – for instance, cruelty, broken homes, and emotional neglect.

The first and third groups, it will be seen, consist of very similar cases looked at from two different points of view: which class they are placed in depends on whether we emphasize chiefly the maladjustment of the child or the unsuitability of the home.

It has already been remarked that in the early years of the child-guidance movement workers were apt to remove children from their homes too lightly, that in some quarters the whole movement had come into bad odour for this fault, but that methods are now changing. Many leading workers today regard the removal of a child as a last resort and a confession of failure, for what removal by itself can never do is to solve the underlying emotional conflict. Too often the results of such a policy are to hide the real problem and to create new ones. Moreover, only two outcomes are possible: either long-term care has to be provided, which is known to be both difficult and expensive, or else the child has sooner or later to be returned to the same conditions from which he came. These long-term considerations are too often ignored in face of the temptation to use a relatively easy short cut. Only if the social worker, the doctor, or the magistrate has a well-considered long-term plan for a child is it permissible to remove him from his home for his own good. Without such a plan his removal is merely the creation of yet another deprived child.

But even if great caution is exercised in removing children from their homes, and even if far better measures are introduced to prevent children becoming maladjusted, there will be a need for many years to come to care for many maladjusted children away from their homes. Though many with less obvious difficulties and even some delinquents may be handled in foster-homes, it is widely agreed that the majority of the more aggressive and delinquent characters must first be helped to a better social adjustment. How is this to be done and in what conditions?

A variety of residential accommodation will be necessary if all children – those of different ages and with different disturbances – are to be catered for. This book will do no more than describe certain general principles to be followed when dealing with children aged six years and over.

First, all the conditions described for institutions in general apply. Children must be split into small groups, which are best housed in separate cottages or flats, with their own house-mother or father. Sometimes cottages will be grouped together as a 'village'. At others they will be scattered over a limited area. Each plan has its advantages, the main one of the scattered arrangement being that each hostel or cottage can develop its own private way of living according to the personalities of the house-parents and without awkward comparisons being made by the children.

In regard to the mixing of sexes and ages, there are considerable differences in practice; in the case of maladjusted children the tendency is towards separating younger children from adolescents, and separating the sexes also once adolescence is reached. Not all would accept the desirability of these divisions, however. But there is no difference of opinion regarding size of group: all agree it must be kept small. Probably the best size depends largely on the age of the children for whom provision is being made. The younger the fewer is a sound principle. In any case, none of those professionally concerned recommends more than about sixteen children in a cottage, even in the case of adolescents, and the maximum of twenty-five suggested by the British Ministry of Health on the basis of experience with wartime hostels for difficult children cannot be approved of. For such a number is too many if any curative treatment is to be tried, unless, of course, it is broken up into sub-groups, each with its own house-parents.

As in the case of normal children, maladjusted children must be kept in touch with their parents, both by receiving visits from them and by making holiday visits to their homes. Moreover, there is the same need for case-work with parents – a need too easily neglected – and for a properly considered long-term plan, in the making of which the child and his parents should take part.

Because of the necessity of closely working with both parent and child, treatment centres should only take children from within a reasonable distance of the centre, which means that such centres must be scattered widely throughout a community.

All are agreed that the success or failure of the centre will turn on the personalities of the house-parents; here are wise words on their selection:

> We find that the nature of previous training and experience matters little compared with the ability to assimilate experience, and to deal in a genuine, spontaneous way with the events and relationships of life. This is of the utmost importance, for only those who are confident enough to be themselves, and to act in a natural way, can act consistently day in and day out. Furthermore,

wardens are put to such a severe test by the children coming into hostels that only those who are able to be themselves can stand the strain.

But though the writers of this and also the British Ministry of Health have been inclined to regard previous training and experience as of secondary importance, this is probably because hitherto there has been no training which has been of much use for the work to be done. Once it is recognized that the task is one of making skilled human relationships with children who have had their capacity to do this greatly injured, the need to train house-parents, practically as well as theoretically, in the psychology of human relations and of child development is evident. This work must certainly be professionalized – just as nursing has become professionalized – and all workers must become proficient in the principles and practice of mental health. Only with such training is it possible to expect them to tolerate the three symptoms which all must understand – hostility, grief, and babyish behaviour – and to acquire skill in handling them. And not only must the house-parents understand these things, they must also be able to teach their domestic staff about them, since in a small unit all must follow similar principles and the relations of the children to the domestic staff are of the greatest importance.

The children's need to test the hostel staff, to see if they really are good and really can tolerate and manage their aggressiveness and greed, has been discussed as follows:

> Each child, according to the degree of his distrust, and according to the degree of his hopelessness about the loss of his own home (and sometimes his recognition of the inadequacies of that home while it lasted) is all the time testing the hostel staff as he would test his own parents. Sometimes he does this directly, but most of the time he is content to let another child do the testing for him. An important thing about this testing is that it is not something that can be achieved and done with. Always somebody has to be a nuisance. Often one of the staff will say: 'We'd be all right if it weren't for Tommy . . .', but in point of fact the others can only

afford to be 'all right' because Tommy is being a nuisance, and is proving to them that the home can stand up to Tommy's testing, and could therefore presumably stand up to their own.

Because of this type of behaviour and because of the intensely personal relationships necessary, it is widely recognized that house-parents must be given the choice of accepting or refusing a child. A warm personal relationship with tolerance of much difficult behaviour cannot be provided to order. Moreover, each pair of house-parents will find one sort of difficulty easier to handle than another. For these reasons the policy of organizing groups of hostels, permitting each to be a little different, has much to recommend it.

Much has been written on methods of discipline in treatment centres of this kind. All are agreed that methods must be informal and relatively free and based essentially on close personal relationships between grown-ups and children instead of on impersonal rules and punishments. Democratic methods in which the children themselves play a great part in the control of the community often prove useful, but they must not be thought of as sufficient in themselves, while several limitations in their use need to be observed. First, the growth of self-government cannot be forced and must be built step by step with the help of adults skilled in community work. Secondly, children under eleven cannot manage self-government, except in minor matters, and should not be exposed to the strain and chaos which is likely to follow if it is tried. Perhaps it is only when the group contains a number of children over fourteen years that anything on a large scale can be made to work. Thirdly, children who have been deprived of a satisfactory early home experience have not the inner resources necessary to enable them to take part in self-government. Self-government is thus no universal cure, though appropriately introduced it can be of great value.

As regards education, it is desirable whenever possible for children to go to the ordinary local schools, but it must be recognized that many of them are too emotionally ill either to benefit from or to fit into such schooling. In these cases tuition must be provided on the premises, which is of course more easily done if the centres or cottages are grouped as a 'village' than if they are scattered.

In this as in other matters, a good deal of flexibility is necessary and rigid administrative machinery which divides schools from hostels is not a good thing.

TREATMENT

So much for the general background for the caring for maladjusted children over the age of six or seven years in groups. What of treatment? It has three aspects:

(*a*) The use of the whole social group for curing the children.

(*b*) The development of a special relation between a child and a staff member.

(*c*) The provision of individual psychotherapy or counselling.

Much has been written as regards the first aspect by those concerned in the development of self-governing communities, which are of especial value for adolescents who are not too disturbed. A different aspect of the value of the group is the way in which other children can by their behaviour to the newcomer help him to get insight both into his behaviour and into his fantasies. The emotionally disturbed child frequently mistrusts things put into words: it is his experiences of what actually happens within the group which often bring him healing.

Probably all would agree that, curative though relations with other children can be, it is the relations with grown-ups which carry the main treatment load. Some workers advocate that the house-parent should give treatment. Others, probably a majority, prefer the roles to be filled by different workers. In the latter case treatment is usually given by the social worker who has handled the case from its beginning, and who has therefore made relations with both child and parents. She may well begin to give such help to a child before he has left home and may continue treatment after he has returned, a plan which a house-parent is unlikely to be free to follow. By so doing she gives a most important continuity.

In all countries there is much debate in medical circles regarding treatment given by non-medical workers, but, though they still have their critics, it is safe to say they have come to stay. Those psychiatrists who have actually had experience of working with social workers and psychologists in this way are almost unanimous regarding their value, though they would emphasize the need for them to be properly trained and to work in close collaboration with a doctor trained and experienced in psychological treatment.

The relation of the child to the person giving treatment and to the house-mother can vary through every kind of maladjusted behaviour – remoteness and refusal of contact, hostility, clinging babyishness, and every combination of them. Of the three, remoteness is the most serious, clinging babyishness the most hopeful, for the basic wish which has been repressed as a result of frustration is the wish for mothering. Once a child has been able to trust a mother-figure sufficiently to permit himself to express this wish and to go back to an infantile relationship, a great step has been taken, though to the uninformed his behaviour may seem deplorable. The meaning of this treatment has been well described by two British workers, who were responsible for hostels for difficult evacuees during the war:

In the majority of cases children who were difficult to billet had no satisfactory home of their own, or had experienced the break-up of home, or, just before evacuation, had to bear the burden of a home in danger of breaking up. What they needed, therefore, was not so much substitutes for their own homes as *primary home experiences* of a satisfactory kind. By a primary home experience is meant experience of an environment adapted to the special needs of the infant and the little child, without which the foundations of mental health cannot be laid down. Without someone specifically orientated to his needs the infant cannot find a working relation to external reality. Without someone to give satisfactory instinctual gratifications the infant cannot find his body, nor can he develop an integrated personality. Without one person to love and to hate he cannot come to know that it is the same person that he loves and hates, and so cannot find his sense of guilt, and his desire to repair and restore. Without a limited human and physical environment that he can know he cannot find out the extent to which his aggressive ideas actually fail to destroy, and so cannot sort out the difference between fantasy and fact. Without a father and mother who are together, and who take joint responsibility for him, he cannot find and express his urge to separate them, nor experience relief at failing to do so. The emotional development of the first years is complex and cannot be skipped over, and every infant absolutely needs a certain degree of favourable environment if he is to negotiate the essential first stages of this development.

At some centres children are given opportunities for highly babyish behaviour, including taking all their food from a baby's feeding bottle. Some American observers give in some detail the case-histories of two children grossly deprived in early childhood who returned to babyish ways before getting better. One boy of ten, who had been brought up in various institutions and had attempted suicide, began after some weeks to behave like a small child to his house-mother –

In baby talk he called her his mother, saying, 'My mamma washes my hands for me. She gets me clean socks.' He asked her to help him dress and to spoon-feed him. He was permitted to experience this primitive child–adult relationship. Two months later, baby talk and desire for spoon-feeding were given up spontaneously and new aspects appeared in his relationship to his house-mother.

Later, however, he went back temporarily once more, and this time discovered a baby's bottle and fed himself from it. This process of taking to infantile ways in order to restart the growth of primary relationships from a new and better basis takes time, so that stays in treatment centres are matters of years not months. This impresses once again the overriding necessity of preventing these conditions from developing.

Finally, the great problem of dealing with severely maladjusted children between the ages of three and six who cannot remain at home must be noted. Group care is clearly unsuitable, and the provision of clusters of small homes where skilled professional foster-mothers can care for them in tiny families of one or two while they receive treatment is probably the answer. This is inevitably expensive, but the returns for money expended on treatment in these early years are so infinitely greater than at any other age that it would almost certainly prove the wisest of investments. Development in this field is called for. It is to be hoped that it will appeal to institutions and foundations in a position to sponsor it.

CARE OF SICK CHILDREN

It will be evident that all the principles for the prevention of deprivation in children apply equally to the physically sick and to the physically fit, yet this has been all too little recognized by the medical profession, and bad cases of deprivation are still to be found in children's hospitals. It is true that leading children's doctors in many countries are alive to the problem, but there remains a great lag in reform. More serious, some doctors are still unaware of the importance of the matter, though their number is dwindling.

Sir James Spence, in his lecture on *The Care of Children in Hospital*, has given a vivid picture of deprivation in children's wards, fully as bad as that to be found in the worst of the large institutions now universally condemned. He deals especially with the isolation, aimlessness, and uncertainty of children in long-stay hospitals. Referring to his service on the Curtis Committee, he says:

> I have had to listen to a great deal of evidence from men and women who spent much of their childhood and adolescence in

these institutions. The sensitive and intelligent witnesses recalled with nightmare memories the long hours of winter evenings which pressed upon them in their adolescence, the aimlessness of their existence, the uncertainty of their future. They had their lessons each day, and raffia work and entertainments, but there was no intimacy with anyone who could explain to them the purport of their illness or encourage them with plans for the future. The fault lies in the form and arrangement of most of these long-stay hospitals. They have been conceived too much as medical institutions and arranged too much as hospital wards.

What are the solutions? As usual, the first must be to keep the children at home whenever possible. In this connexion Sir James writes:

> I have experimented in the domestic care and treatment of children with active abdominal tuberculosis, of children immobilized by orthopaedic appliances, of children with chronic disease which requires frequent observation and examination; and from these experiments I am convinced that too often and too lightly is the decision made to confine children in long-stay hospitals.

In this connexion the remarkable development of home care for chronically ill patients by the Montefiore Hospital in New York may be quoted. This hospital has set out to treat as many patients in their own homes as in its wards, and has organized for this purpose a major department with its own medical and nursing staff, social workers, equipment to send out on loan, motor transport, and a housekeeper service. The medical director claims that this has been an entire success, with especial value to the patient and his family, because the patient can take part in normal family living in spite of the limitations due to his illness. Costs per head per day of care are no more than 25 per cent of what they are in hospital. Although comparatively few children have been treated, since it is not primarily a children's hospital, the same principles apply. Indeed the very fact that almost all children have an adult to care for them at home means that the housekeeper service, which is an indispensable part of the home medical care of many adults, especially women, is less necessary. This pioneer work of the Montefiore Hospital may well lead to a great revolution in hospital practice, and one which, from the point of view of the prevention of children being deprived, would be of the utmost value.

In those cases where children must come into hospital much can be done to lessen the emotional shock. In the case of children under three, Sir James Spence has long advocated whenever possible the admission of the mother with her baby.

I have worked under this arrangement [in the hospitals at Newcastle upon Tyne] for many years, and I count it an indispensable part of nursing in a children's unit. Nor is it a revolutionary idea. By far the greatest part of sick children's nursing is already done by mothers in their homes. Not all illnesses will be suited to this nursing, but the majority of all children under the age of three derive benefit from it. The mother lives in the same room with her child. She needs little or no off-duty time, because the sleep requirements of a mother fall near to zero when her own child is acutely ill. She feeds the child; she tends the child; she keeps it in its most comfortable posture, whether on its pillow or on her knee. The sister and nurse are at hand to help and to administer technical treatment to the child. The advantages of the system are fourfold. It is an advantage to the child. It is an advantage to the mother, for to have undergone this experience and to have felt that she has been responsible for her own child's recovery establishes a relationship with her child and confidence in herself which bodes well for the future. It is an advantage to the nurses, who learn much by contact with the best of these women, not only about the handling of a child, but about life itself. It is an advantage to the other children in the ward, for whose care more nursing time is liberated.

In New Zealand there is a plastic surgery unit for babies and toddlers especially planned with bed-sitting rooms, in which the mothers can nurse their children themselves. Though this is done principally to prevent cross-infection, in which it has been wholly successful, it has had great value for both mothers and babies.

> These babies want mothering more than expert nursing. With their mothers they are happier, more contented, and are able to have more constant attention day and night, and an operation for a contented baby is much more likely to be successful. . . . The mother is just as proud of the result as we are.

Since 1959 this arrangement has been official Government policy in the British National Health Service, and it is planned that all new hospitals for babies and young children will be built on this principle. Fortunately, many of the economically less-developed countries have never forsaken this natural arrangement.

A housekeeper service to care for other children who may be left at home should, of course, be available when required.

Older children who must be admitted to hospital can be prepared for their stay and accompanied to the hospital by their mothers, who will undress them, put them to bed, and see them off to sleep. Nothing is worse than telling a child a fairy tale, perhaps about a party, followed by the sudden disappearance of his mother, leaving the child aghast, either silent or screaming, in the hands of a stranger. Regular daily visiting by the parents is to be encouraged (fortunately it has been found not to increase cross-infection), since it not only increases a child's happiness and sense of security while in hospital, but reduces emotional disturbances after his return. Regular formal visiting hours, it has been found, are a mistake. Instead it is better to encourage mothers to drop in frequently and casually, perhaps when they are out shopping, and stay for fairly short periods, during which they should be allowed to feed and bath their children and to give them small presents.

Though keeping him in touch with his parents must be regarded as the first principle in the psychological care of the sick child, much else can be done for him. Nurses can be assigned to particular children to care for them in all ways, so that each child may feel he has a secure relationship with one real person. Wards can be small, both to make them feel homely and to permit of easy discipline, which is impossible to maintain in a friendly way with large groups of children. There must be far more appreciation of child psychology amongst those administratively responsible for children's hospitals, and it should be some one person's business to provide for the emotional needs of each child. As to discipline, 'punishment is rarely necessary at all, if the nurses have the time and the knowledge to investigate the situation properly, and if they do not go in such fear of higher authority that they themselves become tyrannical'. Experiments would be useful in organizing staff and children in family groups. Sir James Spence, in his recommendations for the reform of long-stay hospitals, writes:

> It would be better if the children lived in small groups under a house-mother, and from there went to their lessons in a school, to their treatment in a sick-bay, and to their entertainment in a central hall. There would be no disadvantage in the house-mother having had a nursing training, but that in itself is not the qualification for the work she will do. Her duty is to live with her group of children and attempt to provide the things of which they have been deprived.

It is necessary to emphasize that these principles apply with equal force to convalescent homes and to psychiatric units for children. If young children are to get the benefits of convalescence without the ill-effects of maternal deprivation they must be sent to homes which accept both mothers and children, as recommended for a different reason earlier in this book. Older children must not be sent so far away that parents cannot easily visit them, while their organization in 'family' groups under house-mothers should become accepted practice. Unfortunately, psychiatric units for children are themselves too often patterned on the old hospital plan of large wards and impersonal corridors. Such units should be situated in buildings like ordinary large houses and run on hostel lines.

Finally, let the reader reflect for a moment on the astonishing practice which has been followed in maternity wards – of separating mothers and babies immediately after birth – and ask himself whether this is the way to promote a close mother–child relationship. It is hoped that this madness of Western society will never be copied by the so-called less developed countries!

CHAPTER 15

Administration of Child-Care Services and Problems for Research

ADMINISTRATION OF CHILD-CARE SERVICES

'FIRST and last, our concern is with the family as an important primary group, of which the child is or was a part.' Any administrative structure which fails to recognize this is in danger of doing more harm than good. The authors of the above quotation, writing more than thirty years ago, conclude:

The failure of agencies, both public and private, as also of juvenile courts, training schools, etc., to lay proper stress on the fact that they are dealing with individuals who are members of families, is one answer why much of the work done for these children is unsuccessful.

Unfortunately it is still true that a notable weakness in the work of child-placing agencies is the lack of constructive case-work with the families of the children concerned. Delay in the return of the children to their own homes may be the result, or, even more disastrous, the permanent separation of parents and children.

In most Western countries the care of neglected and homeless children has grown up piecemeal, in the face of public apathy, as the result of the single-minded energies of a few devoted people. A multitude of private charities has thus arisen, originally devoted to providing food and shelter for children who might otherwise have died. Though the result is patchy and inadequate, this record should not be forgotten and, in criticizing the way in which these ancient charities and large institutions have been run, the devoted service they have given while the public at large stood idly by must be remembered.

Recent years, however, have seen a clear tendency towards uniting the many private charities and societies and setting up services of a general kind. In the U.S.A. family welfare associations and agencies for placing children have sometimes combined with advantages to both. Unfortunately, this merging of child-placing services and family services has not always occurred in the welfare states. For instance, in Great Britain, where as a result of governmental authorities taking responsibility for the homeless child there has been a great revolution in the child-care services, they were until 1964 more or less divorced from family services. This was the direct result of the Curtis Committee, whose advice the Government accepted, having been confined to considering the symptoms – homeless children – and having been, by its restricted terms of reference, curbed from studying the more profound social disturbances lying behind these symptoms. As a result for many years a confused situation persisted in which no one authority had clear responsibility for preventing the neglect or ill-treatment of children in their own homes or of preventing family failure. Yet, as all administrators know, divided responsibility means inaction.

Thus the first two lessons to be drawn from these experiences are:

(*a*) Family welfare and child welfare are the two sides of a single coin and must be planned together.

(*b*) Responsibility for both must be clearly defined and united.

A third principle which has been touched on many times is that:

(*c*) Family and child welfare is a skilled profession for which workers must be thoroughly trained.

A child-care service should be first and foremost a service giving skilled help to parents, including problem parents, to enable them to provide a stable and happy family life for their children. It will also care for the unmarried mother and help her either to make a home for her child or arrange for his adoption, help to get relatives or neighbours to act as substitutes in an emergency, provide short-term care in necessary cases while working towards renewing normal home life, and finally provide long-term care where all else fails. Only if it has legal and financial powers to do all these things, together with social workers trained to carry them out, can a service do its work efficiently. As regards staff, it will require specialists as well as general practitioners – specialists in putting problem families on their feet, specialists in adoption, specialists in long-term care, to name but a few – but it would be a mistake for specialism to be carried too far or for each type of specialist to lose touch with the others. For all are concerned with the same essential problem and all are dependent on the same basic sciences – sociology and the psychology of human relations. By working together as partners in a family and child-care service, cooperation in thought and practice can be brought about.

In all these respects the recommended path may be likened to that which medicine has followed over the past centuries. At first there was piecemeal charitable provision for the sick and needy, often little more than just housing them, though as time progressed treatment for common illnesses was added. The great revolution in medicine did not occur, however, until the causes of certain illnesses came to be known and broad preventive measures became possible. Though curative and preventive medicine are still too often divorced from one another, there is a growing recognition of the need for unified health services largely run by professional workers trained in the medical and allied sciences. It is to be hoped that progress in family and child welfare will follow a similar course. Where voluntary agencies are at present giving only a part of these services, especially where they are providing care for children away from home while taking no steps to prevent their removal or to reconstruct the family, they should consider a complete overhaul of their programme. Where government services are planned, it is essential that they should cover the whole problem and be given full responsibility for helping children within their families as well as outside them.

Throughout, this book has stressed the all-importance of parental care for the preservation of mental health. It is, therefore, apparent that family and child-care services must in future be closely associated not only with each other, but with mental health services; for the ultimate aims of all three are the same, their methods are growing more alike, their activities are becoming inextricably intertwined, and each is able greatly to aid the other. The mental health worker and the child-care worker must learn to work together. For this to be effective, changes will often be required in both. Not only is it necessary for child-care workers to be as well up in the principles of mental health as they already are in the principles of physical hygiene, but mental health workers must take the trouble to learn far more than they now know about the problems of families and children and about the work of those concerned with their welfare. Only if a psychiatrist, a psychologist, or a psychiatric social worker is really familiar with day-to-day conditions is his advice likely to be useful. It is for this reason that the best work is now being done by family and child welfare agencies, which have as staff members workers trained in mental health or which have been wise and fortunate enough to appoint psychiatric consultants who give much time and thought to the work. Only by such constant cooperative effort towards a common goal is it possible to develop the mutual respect and understanding necessary for success. The occasional sending of isolated cases to a psychiatrist busy with other problems is futile and apt to breed ill-will on both sides.

RESEARCH INTO METHODS OF PREVENTING MATERNAL DEPRIVATION

There is hardly a topic touched on in the second part of this book around which there is not a shroud of ignorance. Here and there, thanks to the patient and painstaking work of an individual, there is a chink of light, but for most of the time the investigator must fumble in the dark, guided, if lucky, by the carefully formulated but untested theories of the observant worker, and at the worst confused by crystallized tradition and unwitting prejudice. These are not the conditions which make for effective and economic measures for preventing deprivation in childhood, nor are they the conditions which have led to the triumphs of the sister science of preventive medicine. There will be no triumphs in preventive mental hygiene to compare with diphtheria immunization or malaria control without sustained and systematic research carried on over a long period and in many countries.

Though much of this research will necessarily be connected with the pros and cons of different practical measures, there are certain basic theories which need testing; the first being that the grown-up's capacity for parenthood is dependent in high degree on the parental care which he received in his childhood. If this proves true, with its sister statement that neglected children grow up to become neglectful parents, understanding of the problem will be far advanced. This theory, if proved true, would greatly simplify the understanding of a great field of behaviour that otherwise seems to be hopelessly complex, complicated, and often contradictory. In an understanding of maladjustment in marriage, of problem parents, promiscuity, and illegitimacy, with all their attendant neglect and rejection of children, this theory is basic.

Even if it is proved true, however, as all the evidence at present suggests it will be, there remain many other factors – economic, social, and medical – which lead to children becoming deprived. As regards the social aspect, studies are required on the different patterns of family life and association, especially the forces which cause some families to live as isolated units unconnected with relatives and neighbours, and others to become parts of larger social groupings from which they get, and to which they give, support.

In addition to these basic studies in personality development and social organization, the results of which might be expected to hold true for all societies, surveys are required in each community to determine the number of children suffering from deprivation and the nature and relative influence of each of the known factors. Such surveys would seek to discover (*a*) the causes of the natural home group's being unable to provide care for the children, and (*b*) the reasons why relatives are unable to act as substitutes. To be useful they would need to be very detailed and to cover, moreover, all the children in the community and not merely those who had come to the notice of the authorities or agencies, since, unless they did so, children neglected in their own homes and children living with relatives would be excluded. To take account of the age of the child, the social and economic class of the parents, and similar conditions requires special skill in survey methods, as well as in social case-work, medicine, and sociology. For these reasons they would probably need to be undertaken by a university or a government department.

Research is also urgently required into the most suitable method of caring for children outside their own homes. Only by constant study of their results can confidence be had in methods, and it is sad that there have been so few large-scale follow-ups of children brought up outside their own homes. It is hoped that this neglect will be speedily rectified and that voluntary agencies and government departments will compete with each other to provide the most accurate and comprehensive facts.

Unfortunately, there are serious difficulties in judging the degree of success of different methods of care; especially is it difficult to find reliable standards of success or failure. This book has many times pointed to the apparent adjustment of children in institutions or foster-homes which has been belied by subsequent events. One notorious mentally unstable English murderer was, while receiving training in an approved school, so highly regarded that he was made the equivalent of head boy! Short-term observable behaviour cannot, therefore, be accepted as a satisfactory standard unless it is recorded systematically and in detail by an experienced observer who knows what to look for. In addition, it is necessary to use (*a*) psychological tests which give evidence about personality at a more profound level, and (*b*) long-term follow-up studies. In using the follow-up method, it is especially important to note the individual's skill as marriage partner and parent, since there is so much reason to fear that present methods of caring for children away from home fail in this all-important respect.

Lastly, it must be recognized that not only is research difficult but there is often active or passive resistance to its being undertaken. Sometimes trustees and officials are inclined to protect the work which they have established and the traditions which they have inherited and cherished. As a result, difficulties, real and imaginary, are brought forward – conditions, it is said, have changed since these children were cared for; it is unfair to submit them to an inquisitorial follow-up; and in any case, remember, they were of bad heredity! These defensive arguments, the weakness of which has been shown, are the result of fear, a fear which springs from the expectation that the research worker will be no more than a hostile critic. The solution, of course, lies in the researcher cooperating in the work of the society in such a way that the people who are actually engaged in it feel they will benefit from his findings.

Part III

FURTHER RESEARCH INTO THE ADVERSE EFFECTS OF MATERNAL DEPRIVATION

BY

MARY D. SALTER AINSWORTH

CHAPTER 16

Controversial Issues

MUCH productive research has followed the strong stimulus of Bowlby's original report to the World Health Organization in 1951. These last thirteen years of activity have shown clearly that research into the effects of maternal deprivation is both difficult and complex, and that some of the problems and findings are not as simple as they may have seemed. The findings of different kinds of research study have been varied, and the conclusions drawn from them have sometimes been divergent and conflicting.

The controversy about the effects of maternal deprivation, nevertheless, is much more a controversy of opinion than of research facts. Indeed, the research findings, when viewed in perspective, form a complex but coherent body of interlocking facts that has many gaps but no inherent contradictions. Since several points have been raised as controversial, it is hoped that these additional chapters will help to clarify them. Eight controversial issues are discussed.

The Question of Definition of Maternal Deprivation

The term 'maternal deprivation' has been applied to several different sets of conditions, which, singly or in combination, sometimes appear to have similar consequences. This has led to difficulty. One such set of conditions has been much explored, namely deprivation that occurs when an infant or young child lives in an institution or hospital where he has no major substitute mother and where he receives insufficient maternal care, and as a consequence has insufficient opportunity for interaction with a mother-figure. Another set of conditions has been less systematically explored, namely the deprivation that occurs when an infant or young child lives with his own mother, or a permanent substitute mother, but receives from her insufficient care and has with her insufficient interaction. In both these circumstances maternal deprivation consists of *insufficiency* of interaction between the child and a mother-figure.

Another set of conditions that is often included under the general term 'maternal deprivation' is mother–child separation. Yet it does not follow that separating a child from his mother necessarily entails that he will then experience insufficient care and interaction. Mother–child separation *may* provide the occasion for such when a child goes to a setting, institutional or otherwise, where he has insufficient interaction with a substitute mother. Provided a child is offered a substitute mother with whom he can sufficiently interact, however, a separation experience need not have this result. Nevertheless, all separation experiences tend to be distressing to a child old enough to discriminate his mother from other persons and to have formed an attachment to her, yet not old enough to maintain this attachment while parted from her. It is thus possible to distinguish *discontinuity* in a relationship from insufficiency of interaction. Because of the distress they bring, discontinuities in attachments may have adverse effects on development, but these effects are not necessarily the same as the effects of insufficiency. Some confusion has arisen, however, both because discontinuity and insufficiency often occur together and also because repeated breaches of ties with mother-figures may have adverse effects which appear rather similar in nature and magnitude to the effects that follow severe and prolonged insufficiency of interaction.

Finally, the term 'maternal deprivation' is used sometimes to cover also nearly every other kind of interaction between mother and child that is believed to have an unhealthy outcome, for example, rejection, hostility, cruelty, over-indulgence, repressive control, lack of affection. Since such forms of interaction need entail neither insufficiency of interaction nor discontinuity of relationship it is proposed that the term *distorted* be used to describe them.

The complexity of conditions that have been included under the term 'maternal deprivation' has been an understandable source of confusion to many. If such confusion and consequent unproductive controversy is to be avoided, distinctions should in future be maintained between (*a*) *insufficiency* of interaction implicit in the notion of deprivation; (*b*) *distorted* relations, without respect to the quantity of interaction present; and (*c*) *discontinuity* of relations brought about through separation. Because all of these have been included by loose custom under the term 'maternal deprivation', in what follows all three are discussed.

The Question of 'Multiple Mothers'

Bowlby's emphasis on the desirability of continuity in the relations between a child and his mother (or substitute mother) and on the importance of a quantity of interaction sufficient for him to be able to form an attachment to this figure has been interpreted by some (for example, by Margaret Mead) to imply that he believes that any dispersion of maternal care among a number of figures has an adverse effect. Perhaps no one would deny the value of continuity in whatever mothering arrangements are made for the care of a child. To say that continuity is needed, however, does not imply that an exclusive pair-relationship between mother and child is essential or even desirable. Bowlby has in fact advocated that the care given by a mother should be supplemented by care from other figures – father,* older sisters and brothers, relatives, and

* Although in the earliest months of life it is the mother who almost invariably interacts most with a child, and to whom a child usually displays his first attachment, usually the father is also a significant figure. While maternal deprivation has preoccupied investigators for the past thirty years, paternal deprivation has received scant attention. Moreover, in many instances where the term 'maternal deprivation' has been used – for example, in institutionalization – the term 'parental deprivation' would have been more accurate, for the child has been parted from both

others. He has also emphasized the desirability of a child's becoming accustomed to care from specific substitute figures in advance of a separation from his mother, whenever a separation is anticipated.

The Question of Variability in the Degree of Damage following Deprivation

Maternal deprivation in infancy and early childhood has been found to result in very varying degrees of impairment. Much of the variation can probably be explained by differences in the form or severity of the experiences themselves. Some of the disparity between findings with respect to degree of damage, however, is an artefact of the level of observation employed. Not all damage is gross enough to be obvious at a crude level of observation. Often enough appreciable damage can be detected only at the more refined level of observation provided by quantitative tests, clinical appraisal techniques or other well-controlled observations of behaviour. For example, a group of deprived children may be found significantly inferior to non-deprived children in language ability when standardized tests of language are used, although their inferiority may not be apparent merely from listening to their talk. Even when careful appraisal is undertaken, however, some deprived children are found to be affected more adversely than others who appear to have had much the same experience, while some emerge with little or no apparent damage. The fact that some seem to escape relatively unscathed has led some critics to question the validity of the proposition that maternal deprivation is pathogenic.

As Bowlby has pointed out, however, a parallel may be drawn with the effects of infectious disease. The fact that some children escape illness despite being exposed to a

---

parents and deprived of interaction with a father as well as with a mother. It is to be hoped that future research will give more adequate attention to the influence of father–child interaction on the course of development.

disease-producing organism neither disproves that the organism can cause the disease nor suggests that, if it is a disease that may have serious adverse effects, we should condone the exposure of other children to the organism. That exposure to maternal deprivation does not result in severe damage to all children has none the less led some people to conclude that it is not the cause of the impairments that are observed in many, and that something else must be responsible.

The Question of Specific versus General Effects of Deprivation

Maternal deprivation has a differential effect on different aspects of human functioning. Although prolonged and very severe deprivation during infancy may at the time affect so many psychological processes that the child seems totally retarded, even then, on close examination, some processes are found to be more severely affected than others. (The age of a child at the time of onset of deprivation seems to be important in determining which processes are impaired and to what degree.) Inevitably researches that differ with respect to the processes examined will yield disparate findings. Thus, one study may examine general intelligence, another language ability, another the character of interpersonal attachments, and still another habit disorders such as thumb-sucking and bedwetting; yet some critics have concluded that, if deprivation results in no adverse effect on the particular process they have selected for study, no damage has been done. The assumption that deprivation affects all processes in equal degree has been a major source of misunderstanding and hence of controversy.

The Question of Diversity in the Nature of the Adverse Effects of Deprivation

The effects of maternal deprivation have been found to be diverse in nature as well as in degree. Some of these diversities obviously can be explained by the great diversity of antecedent experiences that have been included under the term 'maternal deprivation'. But even the same class of deprivation experience may result in disparate effects on the same process in different children. Thus, for example, the processes through which interpersonal ties are established and maintained may be affected, but one child may emerge as detached and 'affectionless' while another may cling anxiously to his mother and be over-dependent on her. The paradoxical nature of different outcomes has led some critics to be sceptical that they could all stem from the same cause.

The Question of Permanence of the Effects of Deprivation

The claim made by Bowlby, Spitz, and others that severe, early deprivation of maternal care may have *permanent* effects has led to sharp controversy. Some critics who acknowledge that young children are impaired while undergoing deprivation are none the less reluctant to concede that an early experience can lead to permanent damage that cannot be eliminated by favourable influences later in life. This controversy has been facilitated by several considerations of which the most important seem to be: (*a*) even a severely damaged child may improve to some extent if deprivation is relieved; (*b*) impairment of some processes seems more susceptible to improvement than impairment of other processes; (*c*) some damage is more obvious and more easily observable than other damage that may nevertheless be more resistant to change; and, finally, (*d*) it is very likely that some lasting effects are apparent only in special circumstances – perhaps much later in life – which reactivate and make manifest unhealthy processes originally set in train by early deprivation but which remain hidden until this later time. Inadequate attention to these points has misled some critics.

The Special Question of Delinquency

Particular controversy has centred upon delinquency as an outcome of maternal deprivation. Bender applied the term 'psychopathic behaviour disorder' to the clinical syndrome she found associated with early and severe deprivation experiences. An early study of Bowlby's used juvenile thieves as subjects, and demonstrated an association between the 'affectionless character' shown by some of the most persistent of them and early, severely depriving separation experiences. Bowlby suggested that experiences of this nature may be foremost among the causes of 'delinquent character formation'. These and similar findings and opinions of other early investigators, have led to the widely held belief that the hypothesis that maternal deprivation causes later maladjustment or disorder necessarily implies that deprivation always or frequently causes delinquency. As it turns out, delinquency has not been found to be a *common* outcome of maternal deprivation or early mother–child separation; and this has led some critics to conclude that deprivation itself is not damaging.

The Question of 'Maternal' versus 'Environmental' Deprivation

Among those who accept the evidence that the effects of institutional care of infants and young children are generally adverse there is controversy about whether the ill-effects are attributable to the absence of a mother-figure or to deprivation arising from a relatively low level of environmental stimulation in the institution setting. Those who inculpate 'environmental deprivation' tend to be hard-bitten scientists who feel uneasy about what they hold to be a mystic aura in the words 'mother' and 'motherly care'. They want to be sure that no one believes that there is anything magic about a mother, over and above her behaviour and the stimulation it gives a baby. They would prefer to dissect the baby's environment, including the mother, into clear-cut, measurable variables and to dispense with the mystique. Such an approach is necessary to the extent that it helps to ascertain what the factors are in a mother's care of her baby which are lacking in institutional care and which are necessary for healthy development. On the other hand it hinders understanding to the extent that it is a flight from a recognition of the importance of interpersonal relations and that it represents an attempt to understand a baby's world solely or mainly in terms of stimulation arising from the physical environment.

The next chapter considers each of these points of controversy in the light of research evidence, giving attention both to the interacting variables that are present in the deprivation experiences studied and to the research strategy and methods of data collection that are used. When viewed in these wider contexts, there seem to be no serious contradictions between findings. If the evidence is so coherent, the reader may well ask why controversy has arisen.

Reasons for Controversy

Some controversy seems to be due to misunderstanding, oversimplification or distortion of the findings and conclusions of earlier work. Although such misunderstandings and distortions may seem preposterous at first glance, they can be understood when one considers the tremendous complexity of the texture of the human condition.

Thus, some unnecessary controversy stems from inadequate recognition that both 'maternal deprivation' and 'mother–child separation' are terms that cover many kinds of experience, differing greatly in severity, and that the effects of these experiences depend on a multiplicity of variables. These variables have been discussed in detail elsewhere. They include: the age of the child at separation; the nature of his experiences (including his experiences with his mother) before separation; the duration of the separation; the extent to which substitute mother-figures are present to interact with him; the presence of traumatic circumstances either surrounding the separation itself or complicating the experience following separation; and, finally, the nature of the child's experiences after the period of separation is over. Similar variables may be assumed to have significance for children experiencing insufficiency of interaction with their own mothers – or distorted relationships – without separation. It is impossible to give too much stress to these variables. Many seeming inconsistencies between studies are due to a disregard of these sources of variance, either when planning the study or when interpreting the findings, or both. Moreover, in these variables there is implicit great significance for the practical applications of the research results.

Some of the controversy is due to critics supposing that a single complex of experiences, more or less prolonged, occurring in infancy or early childhood, is thought to have a uniform and lasting effect in all cases. Plainly this could not be so. Development of the individual person is an unbroken process. A deprivation experience acts through its influence upon on-going processes of development, and is interpreted in the light of previous experience. The on-going processes upon which it acts are, in turn, a result of the whole previous history of development that has taken place through the interaction of the person (and his genetically determined hereditary structure) with the influences pressing on him from his environment. The response to relief from deprivation is determined both by the processes set up in the course of the deprivation experience and by the extent to which they are reinforced, modified, or reversed by later interaction of the person with his environment. All of these influences are important in determining the eventual outcome. Indeed, a vicious spiral starting with and exacerbating the effects of a severe deprivation experience is not uncommon: the processes set up by deprivation make it difficult for a child to respond adequately to the later advances of a mother-figure; the mother, in turn, tends to interact less with such a child than she would with a more responsive one, or perhaps tends to reject him; in this way, a mother may unknowingly reinforce the processes set up during the original experience. Similarly, a child who has been damaged by unfavourable experiences at home before admission to an institution may be more neglected in the institution than a child with a happier previous experience. But to find that pre-separation and post-separation experiences influence the effects of separation is not to say that the depriving separation experience itself has a negligible influence on outcome.

Finally, some of the controversy seems to stem from the complex and difficult problems implicit in research into the effects of maternal deprivation. Various research strategies are available, each with its own strengths and deficiencies, which set limits on the kind of findings and interpretations each can yield. The inappropriate use of a strategy, therefore, can lead to findings that are seemingly in contradiction to the main body of knowledge. This is not, however, the proper place in which to discuss research methodology. The next chapter makes some reference to it, but it is assumed that those readers who are concerned with the details of research will read more widely in primary sources.

CHAPTER 17

Conclusions from Recent Research

An examination of the evidence that has accumulated during the last thirteen years leaves no doubt that maternal deprivation in infancy and early childhood has indeed an adverse effect on development both during the deprivation experience and for a longer or shorter time after deprivation is relieved, and that severe deprivation experiences *can* lead in some cases to grave effects that resist reversal. This conclusion is essentially the same as Bowlby's in 1951. Research both during the last thirteen years and previously, however, makes clear that these adverse effects differ in nature, severity, and duration, and that these differences are themselves related to qualitative and quantitative differences in the deprivation experience. The nature and severity of the deprivation experience are now known to be determined by an interacting and complex set of variables, although much further research is required before the relationship between antecedent depriving conditions and their effects can be specified in detail. In the meantime certain interim conclusions can be drawn, which, in turn, point towards new directions for research.

Diversity of Early Experiences included under the Term 'Maternal Deprivation'

Deprivation conditions very different in kind may none the less lead to effects that appear to be similar in nature and severity. Three diverse conditions are known to lead to severe effects: (*a*) when an infant or young child is separated from his mother or permanent mother-substitute and cared for in an institution where he receives insufficient maternal care; (*b*) when an infant or young child in his own home is given grossly insufficient maternal care by his mother or permanent substitute mother and has no adequate mothering from other people to mitigate the insufficiency of interaction; and (*c*) when a young child undergoes a series of separations from his mother and/or substitute mother-figures to each of whom he has formed attachments.

(*a*) *Institutional deprivation.* The chief evidence of the adverse effect of institutional care comes from the earlier studies and has been reported in preceding chapters. The research of the last thirteen years merely confirms the earlier findings in regard to the general proposition that institutional care is depriving to the extent that adequate substitute mothering is lacking. The details of the later findings will be reported in subsequent sections.

(*b*) *Deprivation at home.* A substantial number of studies reported in the last thirteen years shows that confinement in an institution is by no means the only occasion for deprivation of maternal care. Some of these are individual case studies of severely disturbed children who have been reared by mothers who, for one reason or another, interact insufficiently with their infants. Some are large-scale retrospective studies of separated children which strongly suggest that the degree of deprivation a child has experienced in his own home before separation may have a profound effect on the degree of maladjustment he shows after being separated from his parents. One such study even suggests that very adverse homes may cause severe retardation which can be ameliorated, at least in the older child or young adult, by training in a progressive institution. Some are follow-up studies showing that insufficient interaction with the mother in infancy may lead to impairment still observable in later childhood. These studies make it obvious that mother–child separation is not a necessary condition of maternal deprivation; there can be insufficiency of mother–child interaction without separation and without institutional placement. Deprivation *can* begin at home.

(*c*) *Repeated separations.* The chief evidence for the adverse effect of repeated separations comes from earlier case studies such as those of Bowlby.

Although it is known that these three sets of conditions may lead to effects that are similar in degree of severity, more remains to be discovered about the variations in the effects that can be expected to follow from variations in these three main conditions and combinations thereof. We need more research to help identify the clusters of conditions that lead to more or less severe and lasting effects, and also those that have a mitigating effect.

There is much evidence that the discontinuity of elations brought about by separation from mother or permanent substitute mother (after an attachment has been established and before a child is old enough to maintain his attachment securely throughout a period of absence) is in itself disturbing to a child, regardless of the extent to which separation ushers in a period of insufficiency. The details of these findings will be reported later. We need more research, however, to sort out the influence of discontinuity of mother–child relations from the influence of insufficiency of mother–child interaction. We need to study young children who receive adequate care from a mother-substitute during prolonged separation from their mothers and to compare them with children who have no mother-substitute during otherwise equivalent experiences. Moreover, longitudinal direct studies of infants and young children who undergo repeated separations from their mothers and substitute mothers would do much to clarify the processes by which a series of these experiences results in effects that appear similar to those of prolonged and severe insufficiency of interaction.

It has been suggested that a distinction should be maintained between insufficient and distorted mother–child interaction. Hilda Lewis, whose study of the effects of pre-separation experiences on post-separation disturbance was cited earlier, identified several patterns of distorted parent–child relations which are associated with maladjustment, and found that different patterns are associated with different outcomes. Thus, for example, rejection by parents seems to lead to unsocialized aggression; neglect by parents precedes socialized delinquency; and a repressive regimen is associated with later neurosis. In Lewis's study, however, discontinuity of parent–child relations had occurred in all cases; and insufficiency and distortion were confounded in enough cases to make it uncertain how much weight should be attributed to each of the three factors in contributing to the different patterns of outcome.

Until proved otherwise, it must be assumed that the outcome of a prolonged period of insufficiency of interaction differs from the outcome of a prolonged period in which there is a sufficiency of interaction but of a distorted nature. Although both types of experience may lead to grave effects that resist later reversal, a study of these effects is hindered by confusion between the antecedents. It is difficult enough that often (though by no means always) insufficiency and distortion of interaction go together: for example, the little interaction that a deprived child may have with his mother may be distorted, say, by rejection; whilst a distorted infant–mother relationship may result in a separation experience which itself then brings insufficiency of interaction. In fact, the variables of 'insufficiency', 'discontinuity', and 'distortion' are all too often confounded. Although a major aim of scientific investigation is to differentiate between the effects of variables, research in which the effects of combinations of insufficiency, discontinuity, and distortion are studied is by no means useless. On the contrary, such research should help to identify some of the most adverse of early childhood experiences in which two or three of these variables are combined.

'Multiple' versus 'Supplementary' Mothers

Perhaps because most research into the effects of maternal

deprivation has been carried out in an institutional setting where each child is cared for by a multiplicity of caretakers, it has become commonplace to assume that Bowlby, and others who are deeply concerned about maternal deprivation, claim that any deviation from an exclusive mother–child pair-relationship results in deprivation. It is necessary therefore to distinguish between the following patterns: (*a*) absence of a major mother-figure, and the dispersal of responsibility for the care of a child among a multiplicity of persons, who together give insufficient opportunity for child–adult interaction: this pattern is characteristic of many hospitals and of some residential nurseries and other children's institutions; (*b*) 'serial multiplicity', in which a child is cared for by a succession of substitute mothers, any one or all of whom may give sufficient care, but which results in repeated discontinuity in mother–child relations; (*c*) both multiple and changing caretakers: this is the pattern experienced by a child who has a prolonged stay in a hospital where there is a policy of rotating staff; (*d*) a partial dispersal of responsibility for the care of a child among a few figures who have a high degree of continuity and who together give sufficient care: this pattern exists in many families in which, although the mother is chiefly responsible for the children's care, her care is supplemented by that of certain other members of the household; it is also characteristic of some experimental societies, such as the Israeli *kibbutzim*.

These different patterns have different effects on development according to the degree of insufficiency or discontinuity of maternal care which may accompany them. A multiplicity of mother-figures is often accompanied by insufficient adult–child interaction. In most institutions where each child, in the course of a day, has many caretakers, each adult has partial responsibility for many children. Under these circumstances two factors combine to give insufficiency of interaction: no adult has time to give much attention to any one child; and, since no adult is familiar with the particular behaviour of each child, many of the children's social signals go unheeded. Harriet Rheingold demonstrated that this pattern of caretaking makes for decreased social responsiveness in infants under twelve months of age, even in an institution where the total amount of care given to each child is not obviously deficient. She found that a group of babies to whom she gave intensive mothering, four at a time, for a period of eight weeks became more socially responsive and vocalized more than did a control group of other babies in the same institution who were cared for by multiple figures. After nine months of age all these babies were family-reared, and on follow-up no significant lasting differences were found between the control group and the babies she had mothered intensively (although the latter still tended to vocalize more than the control group). Nevertheless, if insufficiency of this kind is extreme, or is prolonged into the second year of life and beyond, the results can include the grave effects which, by now, are well known.

'Serial multiplicity' is a pattern of infant care found in the 'home management houses' maintained by the home economics departments of some American universities for the training of students in home management, including infant care. Babies stay there for some months, during which they are cared for by a succession of students, each having responsibility for the infant for a few days at a time. This pattern of care might be expected to lead to results somewhat different to those of typical institutional care, for presumably each student gives maternal care that is more or less sufficient, and any adverse effect would be the result of discontinuity. If this pattern of mothering does in fact provide a sufficient amount of adult–child interaction, one would expect social responsiveness to develop but to remain undiscriminating in regard to persons. In these circumstances a child, delayed in forming attachments to specific figures, would, if the discontinuity persists long enough, be expected to develop an 'affectionless' character, incapable of attachment (as sometimes happens in other instances of 'serial multiplicity' – for example, an illegitimate child who passes successively from mother to granny and on to a series of foster-mothers). At the time of writing, there has been but one follow-up study of these children; they were a group who had been cared for as infants in a home management house but who at about ten months of age had been placed in foster-homes and at about twelve months of age had been adopted. These children, when aged from eight to seventeen years, were compared with a matched control group of school classmates in regard to their performance on several paper-and-pencil tests of ability and personality. Although the family-reared control group did slightly better on the tests, they were not significantly different from the group who had experienced serial multiplicity of mother-figures in infancy. Before drawing conclusions, however, it is plainly essential that the capacity for affectional ties of such children be more intensively explored, and also that observations be made both of their reactions to shifts in mother-figure during their first year of life and of the way they later settle in foster and adoptive homes.

Margaret Mead challenges anyone who may believe that an exclusive child–mother relationship is the only satisfactory method of rearing infants and young children; she argues, indeed, that such a relationship might be hazardous for survival under certain conditions. For example, a culture that favours diffusion of care among several figures may well ensure greater continuity of care and less liability to trauma from loss of mother than would occur in a culture that favours concentration of care in the hands of a single mother-figure.

It is right that Margaret Mead should argue for greater consideration of the findings of cultural anthropologists before a pattern of Western family life is assumed to be good for other societies. She concedes that the institutional practices that have grown up in the West as a way of dealing with unwanted children should be considered as a special issue, and she insists that the West should not foist upon non-Western societies an impersonal, insufficient way of caring for such children. A major difference between societies, she points out, is that in primitive societies breast-feeding is essential for survival whilst in Western ones it is not – a fact that makes for inevitable differences in infant-rearing practices.

Several features of Mead's position, however, are challengeable. First, she apparently believes that Bowlby (and others concerned with the adverse effects of early maternal deprivation) sponsors an exclusive mother–child pair as the ideal. This is a serious misunderstanding of Bowlby's position, for he has argued not only that a major mother-figure is desirable (not necessarily the natural mother) but also that her care be supplemented by that of other figures, including a father-figure.

Secondly, she seems to imply that in some non-Western societies successful rearing of infants and children is commonly achieved by a dispersion of maternal care among 'multiple nurturing figures' with no one taking major responsibility. Although such a pattern may be found occasionally, it is not likely to be the norm in any society, especially a primitive one. Indeed, in a society where breast-feeding is the rule, the woman who regularly feeds a child can hardly avoid becoming his major mother-figure.

Thirdly, regardless of the system of infant-rearing common in a given society, it seems entirely likely that every infant tends to attach himself primarily to one specific person no matter how extensive his attachments to other special people. His initiative in attachment behaviour is attested by studies of deprivation in human infants, by studies of sub-human primates, and by a study which the present author conducted in a semi-acculturated African society. If there is indeed a built-in tendency for an infant to attach himself mainly to one specific person, then any situation (whether brought about in an experimental society or by variation in a traditional society) which impedes such attachment might be expected to disturb the normal course of development.

Fourthly, there seems implicit in Mead's argument the view that, if a pattern of child-rearing in a primitive society has survived and can be shown to be a preparation for the life of an adult in that society, it is therefore a desirable mode of child-rearing. Despite the emphasis that she gives to biological factors in survival, her final criterion seems to be the cultural appropriateness of patterns of behaviour. Although this is a common criterion in cultural anthropology, it can be challenged. Can we not differentiate between societies that facilitate and those that handicap the healthy growth of personality – between societies that allow for and those that frustrate basic biological patterns and individual differences therein?

Regardless of these points of difference with Mead's position, it is certainly true that study of non-Western societies is needed – studies of both Eastern European societies (some of which have experimented with new patterns of family life and infant-rearing) and also non-European societies, many of which (whether characterized as primitive or civilized, acculturated or non-acculturated) have patterns of infant-care different from those of Western societies. Interesting questions centre not only on insufficiency, discontinuity, or distortion of maternal care but also on the ways in which the care of a major mother-figure is supplemented, and on the effects of such different child-care methods on a child's development.

Of the various experimental variations in child-rearing, scientific reports of outcome are available for only one – that followed in the Israeli *kibbutzim*. Here, although the daily duration of care given by the natural mother is before long exceeded by that given by the *metapelet*, there is always a known mother-figure present, whether mother, *metapelet*, or her successor, the teacher-nurse in charge of the nursery school. In addition, ties with age-peers are continuous. As Bowlby points out (p. 49), the system entails no abandonment of parent–child relations. On the contrary, all evidence shows that *kibbutz* children make close and meaningful attachments to their parents, but that, perhaps because parents have less responsibility for training in socialization, the attitude of children towards them differs from the attitudes of children reared in the conventional family units of other Western societies.

In contemporary Western societies there are large variations in the amount of supplementary care given to infants. Fathers share in the care of their infants and young children to a greater or less extent, and different households vary in regard to the number and continuity of other supplementary figures: relatives, older brothers and sisters, nursemaids, mother's helpers and baby-sitters, permanent or temporary, full-time or part-time. In Western societies more and more women seem to wish to free themselves from the role of full-time mother and housewife and to share these duties with other people in order to undertake employment outside the home. Whilst attention has been given to the problems of young children whose working mothers are of low socio-economic status, until recently little interest has been taken in the problems of children whose working mothers are of higher socio-economic status.

A recent review shows that, although there has been considerable research into the effects on children of their mothers working, very little of it has been concerned with the effects on infants and pre-school children, or with the effects that different arrangements for supplementary mothering may have. The fact that these points have usually been ignored may be responsible for the general finding that the children of working mothers and the children of non-working mothers do not differ significantly.

The practical problem is not entirely solved by pressing

mothers to delay resuming their careers in order to give adequate care to their infants and pre-school children. As illustrated by case histories of certain severely deprived children, some mothers are unable to provide sufficient maternal care and, therefore, both infant and mother might well thrive better with the mother working and with adequate and continuous supplementary mothering provided for the child. That this is a major issue is demonstrated by the report of a symposium on *Research Issues Related to the Effects of Maternal Employment on Children* in which all contributors emphasize a mother's need to work and all tend to minimize its possibly deleterious effects on infants and young children.

A problem of great theoretical and practical importance for future research, therefore, is to explore the extent to which a major mother-figure can or should share her responsibilities with other figures, with or without continuity, so that we can discover those patterns (and there are probably several) which are favourable for the development of a child's identifications, security, and subsequent mental health. Within such a programme of research it is especially important to explore the effects of a father's relation to his infant and young child, and the effects on subsequent development of different amounts and kinds of paternal care.

Current Studies of Children undergoing Deprivation or Separation

Before continuing to discuss the relevance of recent research to controversies about maternal deprivation, it is desirable to consider some of the findings of recent current studies. Of the studies carried out during the last thirteen years, by far the most numerous have been of separated children whilst undergoing depriving experiences in an institution or hospital setting. Although such studies do not yield direct evidence about long-term effects of such experiences, they are of great value in throwing light on the processes set in train by them, and that must account for whatever long-term effects there may be.

Recent current studies have emphasized the effect of depriving experiences in retarding intellectual development. Thus the early findings of Spitz and Skeels, which once met with severe criticism, have been amply confirmed by subsequent studies; these have shown that deprivation causes retardation of development, that the retardation is progressive as deprivation is prolonged, and that language and social development are the specific processes most severely affected.

Of particular interest is a detailed study by Provence and Lipton which compares the development of seventy-five infants reared in an institution with seventy-five babies reared in families during their first year of life. The motor behaviour of the institution children was not impaired during the first month, and generally motor functions were less retarded than other aspects of development; even so there was retardation in their acquisition of head control, sitting erect, standing, and walking. In particular there was a discrepancy between the acquisition of motor abilities and the infants' use of them as means of adapting to the environment; for example, from the eighth month onwards there was less reaching out for and moving towards people and toys, and reduced use of motor skills for seeking pleasure, avoiding discomfort, initiating social interchange, exploiting the environment for learning, and expressing feelings. Backwardness in vocal behaviour was evident early and became very marked. Although comprehension of language was retarded, it was talking that was most affected. In their reactions to people the institution children were markedly different from the family-reared ones. They were slow to differentiate between people, showed no signs of developing attachment to a specific nurse, and neither developed a sense of trust nor sought help from an adult when in distress. Although an adequate number of toys was provided for the institution babies, they showed little interest in them, no displeasure at the loss of a toy and no effort to recover a lost toy. Spontaneous play with toys was very limited. Altogether their range and intensity of feeling and its expression was greatly impoverished.

Some important current studies have focused on the sequence of responses of infants and young children to separation from mother with concomitant insufficiency of motherly care and interaction. Robertson observed children aged between one and four years undergoing separation experiences in more or less depriving institutional settings, and paid particular attention to the effects that follow disruption of the attachment that a child has with his mother. Three phases of response to separation were observed: (*a*) *protest*, characterized by crying and acute distress at the loss of mother and by efforts to recapture her through the limited means at the child's disposal; (*b*) *despair*, characterized by increasing hopelessness, withdrawal, and decreasing efforts to regain mother, for whom the child is mourning; and (*c*) *detachment*, characterized behaviourally by 'settling down' in the separation environment, accepting the care of whatever substitute figures are available, but with marked loss of attachment-behaviour to the mother when she returns. Believing that these responses, together with the responses to subsequent reunion with parents, could not adequately be accounted for by existing theory, Bowlby has undertaken a reformulation of theory about the origins and development of a child's tie to his mother and a reinterpretation of separation anxiety, grief and mourning, and the defences that follow loss, particularly as they occur in a young child.

The responses to separation described by Robertson are, by and large, confirmed by other studies. One noted protest behaviour in children briefly in hospital for tonsillectomy, and concluded that in children younger than five years anxiety in this situation is related to separation from parents and admission to a strange environment rather than to the operation or anaesthetic. Another observed the reactions to hospital of children between two and twelve years of age, and found that, although all children show some initial disturbance, it is most marked in the group aged between two and four years and is usually clearly related to separation from parents. Aubry and her associates observed the reactions to separation and institutional placement of children in their second year of life, and emphasize the frequency of initial distress as well as the severe disturbances of personality that may result from prolonged separation with inadequate substitute mothering. Heinicke compares children aged fifteen to thirty months newly admitted to a residential nursery with children of the same age newly admitted to a day-nursery and thus separated only part of the day. Children of both groups protested against the separation, but the protest of those in the residential nursery was far greater. Children of both groups had opportunity to form attachments to nursery staff and did so as time went on; but those in the residential nursery formed more intense and ambivalent attachments, were more resistant to adult demands, and were given to more frequent episodes of intense hostility.

Schaffer shows clearly that the response to separation and hospitalization in infants in the first year of life varies with age. Children of seven months and over display the protest pattern typical of children in their second and third years. Babies under seven months, on the other hand, do not protest; instead, they exchange mother for nurses and react to all the other changes in their environment with little overt disturbance. Throughout their stay, however, they are unwontedly quiet, and cry and babble much less than is normal for infants of this age.

Yarrow studied responses to separations that are not complicated by admission to a hospital or institution, namely those that occur when a baby who has been reared by a foster-mother from birth is transferred to an adoptive mother. He found that loss of foster-mother acts as a trauma and results in immediate disturbances of behaviour, such as blunted responsiveness to people, excessive clinging to the new mother, excessive crying, unusual apathy, disturbances in adaptation to routines, sleep and feeding, a drop in the measured IQ, and loss of abilities previously present. The severity and pervasiveness of disturbance was found to increase with age. Of the babies aged three months when separated, only a few showed disturbance; of those who were six months old 86 per cent showed disturbance; whilst every one of the infants who experienced a change in mother-figure at or after seven months of age reacted with marked disturbance. This makes it clear that the breach of a tie once established is in itself disturbing, and that established patterns of behaviour and development are disrupted by it.

The Diverse Effects of 'Maternal Deprivation'

Let us turn now from responses of infants and young children whilst undergoing some kind of deprivation or separation to consider the long-term effects attributable to such experiences. The early studies of deprivation, described in the earlier chapters of this book, emphasize as the outcome of such experiences what Bowlby terms 'affectionless character' – impairment of the capacity to form and maintain deep and lasting affectional ties. Although the cases reported by Bender and Bowlby were not also impaired in general intelligence, the cases reported by Goldfarb were.

The research of the last thirteen years yields a more complex picture and shows that effects may be extremely diverse both in nature and in degree. Beres and Obers carried out a follow-up study of young adults who had spent periods of their early childhood in the same institution as the subjects studied by Goldfarb. Whilst the incidence of severe disturbance remained high, outcome showed greater diversity than Goldfarb had found. This greater diversity they attributed to a longer follow-up of cases into adulthood; but, since their sample was much more heterogeneous than Goldfarb's with respect to age at admission and length of stay (and Goldfarb himself showed these variables significantly to affect the severity of outcome), it remains uncertain whether this is the right explanation.

Bowlby and his associates undertook a follow-up of children who had been admitted to a sanatorium for tuberculous patients sometime during their first four years of life, and who had stayed there for varying lengths of time before returning home to their parents. When tested some years after having returned home they were not found to be significantly less intelligent than a control group of classmates, although they were less capable of concentration and task-involvement and more inclined to withdrawal and apathy and towards roughness and tempers. Although a high proportion of these children were found on follow-up to be more or less severely maladjusted, few of them could be characterized as affectionless. Their personality patterns were diverse, and many showed marked over-dependence.

Stott also found considerable diversity in the personalities of a group of children who had suffered a substantial amount of separation during their first four years of life. His finding that nearly all of them seemed anxious for their mother's approval is comparable to Bowlby's finding of a high incidence of over-dependence.

Recent retrospective case studies also report diversity among adults who had suffered deprivation and/or separation in early childhood. Thus one study of a large number of psychiatric patients shows that those who had suffered separation from mother for at least six months before the age of six years presented diverse symptoms and syndromes. Nevertheless, in this group, disturbances suggesting affectionless character formation (i.e. sociopathic personality disturbances and childhood behaviour disorders) occurred in 27 per cent whereas in the group of patients who had not suffered long separations in early childhood such conditions occurred in only 3 per cent.

Several studies have dealt with childhood bereavement as a special class of separation experience. Loss of one or other parent by death during early childhood is found to have occurred significantly more frequently in the case of mental hospital patients than in the general population. Whilst loss of mother by death before the age of five is found as an antecedent in a number of different psychiatric disorders, it is significantly more frequent among patients suffering depressive reactions than among other groups of patients. That depressive states are an outcome of early separation was not suggested by the earlier studies and is a finding of profound significance. In the first place, it suggests that the effects of early separation can be hidden and not emerge until later in life, perhaps when some repeated experience of loss reactivates the processes that were set in train by the early loss. Secondly, Bowlby attaches particular significance to studies reporting an association between childhood bereavement and later depressive illness because of the similarity he discerns between grief and mourning in an adult and the 'despair' phase of response to separation in a young child. He advances the hypothesis that the defensive detachment which succeeds despair when a young child suffers a depriving separation for a prolonged period precludes a healthy working through of grief and predisposes him to later depressive reactions.

Two retrospective studies attempt to identify some of the antecedent conditions that make for greater or less impairment. Trasler dealt with children placed in foster-homes, comparing a group of children who failed in their foster-home with a group who succeeded there. He found that 56 per cent of the failures were due to the effects of previous separation from the parents – effects attributable to feelings of rejection which had generated tension, anxiety, and lack of responsiveness. This group includes a subgroup (30 per cent of the failures) in which the failure was specifically due to the child being unable to respond to the overtures of the foster-parents. Affectionless detachment, feelings of rejection and consequent aggression seemed especially likely to develop if a child had been in an institution between leaving his own parents and being placed in a foster-home. Trasler concludes that young children tend to interpret separation from their parents as the withdrawal of affection, and that this causes difficulty in subsequent attachment to caretakers. For a child under three years of age, he believes, the disturbance attributable to separation can be transitory if the child is provided immediately with an opportunity for interaction with an individual mother-figure; but it tends to be more severe and lasting if instead he experiences the insufficient interaction characteristic of institutional care.

Kellmer Pringle and Bossio selected, from among institution children who had undergone prolonged separation from their parents before five years of age, two groups of children, one severely maladjusted and one notably stable. The maladjusted children had mostly been separated before twelve months of age and had experienced lasting parental rejection. The stable group had mostly been separated after two years of age and had not been rejected by their parents, but instead had maintained a lasting relationship either with parents or with parent-substitutes.

In conclusion, very diverse effects have been found to follow early childhood experiences coming under the general head of 'maternal deprivation'. Whilst some of this diversity is attributable to the fact that insufficiency, discontinuity and distortion of interaction have all been loosely classed as depriving, even when attention is narrowed to insufficiency there is still diversity of effect. As one might expect, both the nature and the degree of the consequent disturbance seem to be related to the degree of severity of the antecedent experience; whilst some of the diversity is to be accounted for by the fact that, although the same process or processes may be affected by experiences of varying severity, the overt manifestations of these processes may take differing forms. Of other variables that influence outcome, one of the most important is the child's age at the start of deprivation, for this variable seems to determine which processes are affected. Nevertheless, since deprived children share with non-deprived children great variation of experience, and, to be sure, come into the world with different genetic structures – all of which make for diverse personality patterns – much of the diversity that is found after deprivation is not to be explained by the variables that influence the nature and severity of the deprivation experience itself. Finally, effects seemingly diverse may be artefacts, due to different investigators having observed different processes and used different methods of appraisal, some of which are more sensitive than others.

Specific Processes affected by Deprivation

Certain findings point to the likelihood that maternal deprivation has a specially adverse effect on particular processes. Among intellectual processes, the most vulnerable seem to be language and abstraction. Among personality processes, the most vulnerable seem to be those underlying the ability to establish and maintain deep and meaningful interpersonal relations, and the ability to control impulse in the interest of long-range goals. There is also reason to believe that the particular processes affected are influenced by the age of the child – more accurately, the state of development of the child – at the onset of deprivation; thus, for example, present evidence suggests that deprivation during the first year of life affects language development and abstract functioning (and indirectly IQ) more than does deprivation later on. It seems likely, moreover, that discontinuity of relations, as such, has little lasting effect on general intelligence, and that its chief effect is on the capacity for affectional ties, especially in instances where separation from mother-figures is repeated.

There are important lessons here for future research. First, research which purports to assess the effects of separation or deprivation cannot neglect assessment of those processes known to be most vulnerable to damage. Only by demonstrating that those particular processes are minimally impaired can it be established that any cluster of conditions is minimally depriving. Secondly, longitudinal research into the development of those processes is essential; only when it is known how mother–child interaction facilitates their development can it be understood how insufficient interaction hinders it. Finally, attention needs to be given to the ways in which discontinuity of relationships affects the development of attachment.

Some are damaged; some escape damage

That some children may emerge from a deprivation experience with grave and permanent damage and others may seem to escape any severe or lasting adverse effect is, in part, covered by the above discussion of the diversity of effects of deprivation. Whilst it seems likely that some of the puzzling differences in vulnerability to early deprivation will be explained by future research, even if it cannot do so this would constitute no good reason for discarding the hypothesis that such experiences are pathogenic. Differential vulnerability still unexplained is found for all kinds of illness; and it exists in instances where the chief cause of illness has been identified beyond doubt, for example tuberculosis and poliomyelitis, and even where many of the supplementary factors making for vulnerability or resistance are known. That some individuals are exposed to the disease-producing conditions and escape apparently unscathed is no argument for abandoning preventive measures.

Are the Effects of Deprivation Reversible or Irreversible?

Related to the question of differential vulnerability to deprivation is the question of differential recovery from its effects. The question: 'Are the effects of maternal deprivation reversible or irreversible?' surely must be restated: '*How readily reversible?*' Spontaneously, without relief from deprivation, as some believe possible? Or after the ordinary relief provided by removal from the depriving situation – through reunion with parents, or placement in an adoptive or foster-home? Or after very careful placement to meet the particular needs of the particular child, as some claim? Or with once-a-week psychotherapy? Or with intensive psychotherapy, as others report? *How completely reversible?* Obviously, an improvement of IQ from a defective level of, say, 55 to one of 80 implies some reversibility, but it is perhaps not complete. *With respect to what functions?* Whilst a general measure of intellectual functioning, such as IQ, may recover to the normal range, a person may still show impairment in specific intellectual processes such as language and abstraction. A person may perform competently in earning a living and in ordinary social interaction with friends and colleagues and still betray impairment by failure to meet the more intimate personal demands of marriage or parenthood. *Are there hidden impairments?* Findings both that children who have apparently recovered from a separation experience are particularly vulnerable to subsequent threats of separation, and also that there is an empirical association between childhood bereavement and adult depressive illness, suggest that early experiences may set in train processes that can remain covert for a long time but that can, when reactivated subsequently by some stressful experience (which might well be minor and relatively undisturbing to other people), cause a pathological reaction. When the question of reversibility is re-phrased, therefore – 'How readily and completely reversible are the effects of deprivation, either overt or covert, and with respect to what specific processes?' – the evidence is considerable.

Before presenting this evidence, however, it is useful to consider some of the weighty theoretical issues about the nature of development that are raised. There are three principal theoretical positions:

(1) Psychological learning theory implies that development

is entirely or almost entirely a matter of environmental stimulation. When the appropriate environmental conditions are provided, learning will take place, and what has not been learned earlier can be learned later after appropriate conditions have been introduced. According to this position, a child, initially retarded because of deprivation of environmental stimulation, can eventually catch up, provided that deprivation is relieved and enough time is allowed for learning to take place.

(2) Psychoanalytic theory holds that an early experience can set up certain dynamic processes that become entrenched or engrained and that tend to continue despite subsequent alteration of the situation. Thus early maternal deprivation can be viewed as eliciting defensive processes which serve to insulate a child against the painful frustration that would arise were he to seek interaction with an environment that is unstimulating and unresponsive. Once entrenched, such defensive processes tend to maintain themselves, continuing to insulate the child against interaction even when some new environment would prove supportive, responsive, and helpful were he only able to be receptive. According to this position, reversal depends upon the success of efforts to break down the defensive processes.

The defensive processes described by the psychoanalyst appear to be similar to certain phenomena well-known in the psychology of learning; once well learned, a sequence of behaviour may prove very resistant to change and so constitute a serious block to learning some new sequence of behaviour. This interference by old habits with the learning of new habits is poignantly familiar to the golfer who first learned to slice his drive and now cannot learn to hit it straight.

(3) Theories based on a concept of 'sensitive phase' or 'critical period' derive from developmental studies of animal behaviour. These theories hold that there are phases in the course of development during which, provided

certain environmental conditions are present, a process will develop normally, but, when they are not present, not only will development of that process be arrested but subsequent stimulation cannot (or may only with great difficulty) activate it.

These three positions are not incompatible. It seems entirely likely that some forms of impairment can be overcome through learning after deprivation has been relieved, while other forms resist reversal to a greater or less degree because of the presence of defensive processes or habit patterns that have become engrained. Whether still other forms of impairment may persist because a sensitive phase of development has been passed is an open question. Some formulations of the 'critical-period' hypothesis are not essentially different from the psychoanalytic or 'interfering-habit' positions, for there is evidence that a difficulty in instituting responses not acquired in a critical period is sometimes due to the presence of other responses that interfere with them. It is noteworthy that conditions of extreme and prolonged sensory deprivation throughout the period of a chimpanzee's infancy are found to result in permanent impairment accompanied by structural changes that can loosely be described as atrophy through disuse. Plainly much further research is required, of which some must be on animals because it is unthinkable experimentally to subject human infants to the extreme and prolonged deprivation the effects of which it is necessary to investigate if some of these issues are to be settled. In the meantime, evidence is overwhelming that an organism – whether human or infra-human – develops through a process of constant interaction with its environment, and that to the extent that its environment is depriving its development will be retarded or distorted.

In the light of this discussion the findings of studies on maternal deprivation can be summarized:

(*a*) Under ordinary conditions recovery from a single,

brief experience of deprivation and/or separation is fairly prompt and, with respect to overt behaviour, complete. For example, Robertson reports that, provided a child has not reached the detached phase of response to separation, and particularly if he is still maintaining protest, he responds to reunion with his parents with behaviour that indicates separation anxiety – clinging to his mother more than previously, following her wherever she goes, and becoming very anxious when parted from her however briefly. This pattern of response may occur immediately on reunion, or after a period of delay during which there is either detached strangeness or rejection of his mother. Provided the separation has been brief, however, this increased anxiety tends to disappear after a few weeks. Nevertheless, there is evidence that the child continues to be vulnerable to future threats of separation. The presence of this hidden impairment means, therefore, that reversal is not as complete as appears.

(*b*) Relief from deprivation after even many months of it in early infancy can result in rapid and dramatic improvement both in overt behaviour and in generalized intellectual functioning. Nevertheless, when relief does not occur until about eleven or twelve months of age, vocalization may remain retarded. Until they have been thoroughly examined, moreover, persistent effects on other aspects of intellectual and personality functioning cannot be ruled out,

(*c*) Prolonged and severe deprivation, beginning early in the first year of life and continuing for as long as three years, usually leads to very adverse effects on both intellectual and personality functioning, and ones that resist reversal.

(*d*) Prolonged and severe deprivation beginning in the second year of life leads to grave effects on personality that also resist reversal, but at this age effects on general intelligence seem to be fairly completely reversible. Robertson's observations suggest that, during a depriving separation, if a child remains for a long time in a detached phase, after reunion he does not cling to his parents nor does he regain a normal degree of attachment to them. In a small sample of children who were followed through for fifteen years or so an impaired ability to form and maintain close and mutually satisfying affectional ties tended to persist.

(*e*) Both the age of a child at the onset and his age at the relief of a deprivation experience are undoubtedly important factors in influencing reversibility, but not enough about their effects is yet known to enable precise limits to be set for a 'sensitive phase' of development for any one process. There is evidence, nevertheless, that the period from seven months of age to perhaps ten or eleven months is one during which the infant is especially vulnerable to the disruption of ties newly formed. Spitz found that the effects of a depriving separation beginning in that period and lasting for five months or longer tend to resist reversal, even when measured crudely by IQ; whilst other studies show a reversal of effects, even after longer periods of deprivation, if they begin earlier in the first year of life or else not until after the first birthday. It may be that the period from about seven to eleven months is a sensitive one in human development; if so, it seems likely that the processes most vulnerable are vocalization and language, and also the capacity for personal attachments.

(*f*) In general, during the first year of life, the younger the infant when deprivation is relieved (and hence the less prolonged the deprivation experience) the more normal is subsequent development; after the first year of life has passed, the older the child at the onset of deprivation the more readily and completely reversible seem to be the effects of a deprivation of a given duration.

(*g*) Certain kinds of impairment seem to be less readily and less completely reversible than others; these include impairments in language, in abstraction, and in the capacity for strong and lasting personal attachments.

(*h*) Especially if undertaken when the child is still very young, intensive therapeutic efforts may result in marked improvement of some very severe effects, of a kind that resist reversal by ordinary relief from deprivation.

(*i*) Subsequent experiences of insufficiency, distortion or discontinuity in personal interaction may maintain or increase impairments that might otherwise have been reversed more or less completely.

Prompt and dramatic reversals can be regarded as due to relief from distress or grief or to the sudden giving way of defensive processes that have not yet become entrenched. More gradual and steady improvements are probably attributable for the most part to catching up through learning. A prolonged resistance to improvement is probably attributable to deep-seated defensive processes, or to habit patterns that interfere with the acquisition of new responses, or to the difficulty of activating a development that usually takes place in a sensitive phase now past. Empirical evidence for the existence of a sensitive phase is clearest for language, abstraction, and other symbolic functions. It seems to occur during the first year of life, most probably during the second half of the first year; its upper limit is still uncertain.

The generalizations presented above leave many gaps to be filled through future research. In the first place, far more needs to be known about the normal course of development in the early years of those processes specifically vulnerable to deprivation, especially those that make for personal attachment and those that later blossom into language and the use of symbols. Historically, child development research has focused on children of nursery-school age, namely three years plus, and new-born babies have also been studied intensively. The very period that seems most vulnerable to deprivation, however – the first three years of life – remains largely unexplored, especially with respect to social development. Only in very recent times has there been a quickening of research interest in this period, but, because developmental studies are time-consuming, findings are only just beginning to find their way into print. In the meantime, so long as the normal course of development remains unknown, it is not possible to be precise about the effects of experiences of deprivation in arresting, retarding, or distorting that development.

In the second place, methods of personality appraisal available even for the older child and adult remain relatively clumsy and imprecise. Conceptualization of the processes and variables to be explored is still inadequate, and perhaps will remain so until there is better understanding of underlying developmental processes; meanwhile quantitative appraisal of personality processes is likely to be premature. Inevitably any judgement made about the reversibility of an impairment due to early experience turns on the level at which the assessment is made. The more superficial the assessment – and premature quantification makes for superficiality – the more evidence there appears to be of reversibility; the more intensive, clinical and descriptive the assessment the more evidence there appears to be of lasting damage.

Nothing encourages a sanguine view of the reversibility of impairment caused by early and severe maternal deprivation. Even though some of the effects of deprivation may be reversible somewhat more readily, more completely and more frequently than was thought possible in 1951, there are distinct limits to the improvement that can be expected in cases of severe impairment of long standing. Evidence of covert and subtle effects persisting after even a relatively mild separation raises a doubt, moreover, whether, in cases where deprivation has been early and severe, complete reversibility is possible. Perhaps 'complete reversibility' is an illusory product of crude methods of appraisal.

More research is obviously needed further to delimit the conditions that facilitate reversal and to identify conditions in which deprivation, if unavoidable, is minimally harmful.

Meanwhile the cost of attempting to reverse the effects of early deprivation is very great – so great that every effort should be bent towards their prevention.

Delinquency and Deprivation

The relationship between early separation and/or deprivation experiences and delinquency remains controversial because evidence derived from different sorts of research appears to conflict. Evidence derived from retrospective case studies of psychiatrically disturbed children and adults regularly demonstrates a significant association between, on the one hand, behaviour disorders and character disorders including the 'affectionless' character and, on the other, severe, early, and depriving separation experiences. Thus one study of children in a guidance clinic shows that conduct disorders, including stealing, occur significantly more frequently among children from homes broken by the loss of one parent through death, divorce, or separation than among children from intact homes. When they do occur among children from intact homes, moreover, conduct disorders are more frequent in those who have been separated from their mothers than in other children. Neurotic disorders, on the other hand, are found more frequently among children from intact homes and among children who have not suffered mother–child separation. A particularly interesting finding is that the parents of the two sorts of children also differ in regard to the homes they come from. Children with conduct disorders are more likely to have parents one or both of whom themselves come from a broken home, whereas children with neurotic disorders tend to have parents who come from intact homes. This study supports Bowlby's concept of a vicious cycle. It starts in one generation with a home that may have been accidentally broken by death or illness; as a result the children of the next generation grow up to have difficulties in interpersonal relations and are unable to provide an affectionate, secure environment for their children; as a consequence the third generation develops conduct disorders.

Evidence derived from retrospective case studies of persistent delinquents (whether regarded as psychiatrically disturbed or not) points repeatedly in the same direction. One recent study, for example, found that loss, before a child's tenth birthday, of either (or both) parents through death, divorce, separation, or prolonged absence had occurred twice as frequently in a delinquent group as it had in a matched group of non-delinquents. (Loss of mother was not, unfortunately, distinguished from loss of father.)

Although two other recent studies did not find mother–child separation to be linked with a delinquent outcome, in each of them the sample studied seems to have been so selected that cases of severe personality disorder were excluded. In one of them subjects who had experienced separations due to death, divorce, or separation of the parents were omitted – thus ruling out most of the very sort of deprivation experiences that had led to Bowlby's original findings and to his hypothesis that prolonged mother–child separation in the first five years of life 'stands foremost among the causes of delinquent character development'. On the basis of further work the author of another study has himself concluded that his earlier findings were misleading, and for the same kind of reason. He now holds that the more seriously delinquent the sample examined the higher is the incidence of early separation. This conclusion fits the evidence well.

Evidence from retrospective follow-up studies, however, is more difficult to fit in because, when a group of children who have suffered early, prolonged, and severely depriving separation experiences is followed up, only a very small incidence of delinquent outcomes is found. Lewis's findings link delinquency with parental neglect, and not with separation as such.

It is obvious that there are many different causes of delinquency and that only a proportion of criminal or delinquent acts results from serious defects in character formation such as the 'affectionless' character. If there is to be fruitful research into the validity of the proposition that a special kind of character formation predisposing to persistent delinquency results from some definable kinds of experience in early childhood, certain steps are necessary. First, it is essential to study not miscellaneous delinquents, however anti-social, but delinquents who have been assessed thoroughly enough to be classified according to their character formation. Secondly, it is possible that neither separation nor deprivation alone is the effective antecedent even of the 'affectionless' character, but rather that the antecedent is either repeated separations or some special form of distortion in early parent–child relations, or else, and perhaps more probably, distortion in conjunction with separation or deprivation experiences. Therefore, the need is for an especially thorough investigation of antecedents, with a special study of those antecedent experiences in which distortion, insufficiency, and discontinuity in parent–child relations are combined. Furthermore, it is essential to consider father–child relations as well as mother–child relations. For this kind of exploration, careful retrospective case studies are required.

'Environmental' Deprivation

While psychiatrists, social workers and clinically oriented psychologists have been concerned with the effects of maternal deprivation upon the development of the young human, a number of experimental psychologists have been investigating the effect of various kinds of early experiences on the subsequent development of young animals, such as dogs, cats, white rats, monkeys, and chimpanzees. In particular, they have been interested in depriving the animal of stimulation. It is possible in research with animals both to control the nature of early experience much more precisely than is permissible with human infants, and also to submit them to much more severe deprivation experiences than even the most depriving institution provides for the children who are reared there. An impressive mass of experimental findings is accumulating, which, although containing some apparent contradictions, is gradually leading us towards a greatly improved understanding of the nature of learning during the infancy period and its influence upon subsequent development. It is not possible here to give even a simplified summary of this complex body of findings or of its possible implications for understanding human development.

Arising out of this field of animal research, however, a number of psychologists have been led to suggest that the key factor in 'maternal deprivation' is in reality not the lack of relationship with a mother-figure but something quite different, namely inadequate stimulation from the environment. This has led Yarrow, in a recent review of the literature on maternal deprivation, to emphasize the need for research to analyse the deprivation experience into its components of sensory, social, and emotional deprivation.

While we agree that further research of this nature is highly desirable, and while we agree that, in comparison with the average family environment, an institution environment is often monotonous, barren in emotional tone, and meagre in environmental stimulation, studies such as those by David and Appell and by Provence and Lipton strongly suggest that the most significantly depriving aspect of routine institutional care is insufficient interaction with a mother-figure, and that as a result a child grows unresponsive to the toys provided for him to play with and to the opportunities for activity that even the restricted life-space of an institution offers. In the life of a family-reared infant the chief perceptual stimulation is not so much what comes from the impersonal environment but what comes during periods of interchange with his mother in the course of her caring for, handling, holding, playing with, and talking to him. Thus, in the early months the main cause of 'sensory' or 'environmental' deprivation is insufficient interaction with a mother-figure. It must be remembered, moreover, that the processes most affected by 'maternal deprivation' – the capacity for personal attachments and language – depend for their development on interpersonal interaction. For children over six months of age and throughout the second and third years of life (at least) the most significant single aspect of deprivation in the ordinary institution is the lack of opportunity to form an attachment to a mother-figure, either for the first time or as a substitute for an attachment that has been broken. This is well illustrated by the findings of one of the earliest series of studies of institutional deprivation. Measures to enrich the institutional environment by providing nursery-school experience for children over two years were much less effective in stemming retardation than were measures that gave a child opportunity to attach himself to a substitute mother.

Other Points of Controversy

Critics have sometimes suggested that the effects attributed to maternal deprivation, especially different kinds of intellectual deficit, are in reality due to defective heredity, to organic brain damage or to malnutrition.

Those who blame defective heredity seem to believe that every infant who has no genetic or organic defect will develop normally – with a gradual and inevitable unfolding of his inborn potential – provided only that his basic physiological needs are satisfied. Evidence from animal studies shows this belief to be untenable. So does evidence from studies of human development.

Although some children may be both ill-endowed and also deprived, the dramatic improvement following psychotherapy of some children who are retarded, as well as the slower but still impressive improvements in intellectual level of others noted by Clarke and Clarke, are clear demonstrations that some apparent feeble-mindedness is attributable to defective experience rather than to defective heredity. Similar evidence is provided by the dramatic relief from 'hospitalism' shown by infants after reunion with their mothers. The case against attributing all cases of mental retardation to heredity comes not only from studies of maternal deprivation. There is now a substantial body of evidence which demonstrates beyond question that the development of intelligence is determined by experience, especially early experience, to a degree much greater than has generally been believed. Furthermore, it is gradually becoming recognized in English-speaking countries that the great Swiss scientist, Jean Piaget, has already provided a clear and detailed account of how it is that these early experiences influence the development of intelligence.

Although organic brain damage is, at least in minimal or sub-clinical form, now known to be much more frequent than was previously believed, dramatic improvement following relief from deprivation in some children makes it plain that deprivation, not brain-damage, is the main cause of their condition. It is nevertheless true that the differential diagnosis between constitutional defect, organic brain damage, infantile autism, and retardation attributable to severe deprivation is sometimes a difficult one to make.

As for the possibility that malnutrition may be responsible for the retardation of children in institutions, although diet may be a contributing factor in some, in most of the institutions in which studies have been made the children received an adequate diet and adequate care of other physical needs. Despite this provision severe retardation occurred.

Thus, when viewed with a knowledge of the complex network of variables that influence outcome, the empirical findings of research into the effects of maternal deprivation contain no real inconsistencies. Nevertheless it is clear that there is much yet to be learned. Because of the practical significance of its findings for child care, study of the effects of maternal deprivation has captured the interest and aroused the emotions of many. The attention of others has been caught by the great significance of its findings for an understanding of child development. Deprivation research demonstrates the serious impact on infants and young children of the absence of a mother, even though basic physical needs are met; and this raises the question of how it is that a mother promotes the normal development of a child. The answer obviously lies in the interaction that she has with him. This leads us to ask what we know of the interactions that normally take place between a child and his mother in the period from birth to nursery-school age – that period during which direct study of interpersonal relations has been so sadly neglected. Since early mother-child interaction is a necessary condition for healthy development, and particularly for social development, we need to know far more than we do of how such interaction produces its effects.

Thus, although further research into the theoretical and practical aspects of maternal deprivation is essential to fill the many gaps in our knowledge, further research into those interactions of mother and child that occur in the absence of deprivation may prove even more rewarding. In the study of such interaction, to focus wholly on the mother, either in her caretaking role or in her stimulus-providing role, would be to do only half the job. The very term 'interaction' implies that there is more to an infant than a bundle of needs and responses that passively waits for external stimulation. Just as it is impossible now to believe in an autonomous infant who, given a tolerable environment, develops gradually and inevitably according to a pre-determined blue-print laid down in his genes, so is it impossible to believe in a passive, recipient infant who is infinitely malleable by environmental stimulation. Neither concept is adequate when research turns to mother–infant interaction and its influence on development. The questions that need answering are many. What is the infant's contribution to this interaction? What patterns of behaviour are built into the human organism that may play a part in initiating interaction? How does a mother's response to these forms of behaviour serve to facilitate development? What is the social function of patterns that emerge in the course of motor development and of cognitive development (about both of which more is known than about social development)? In short, how does the inherent structure of the human organism interact with the structure of its environment, and especially its personal environment, to shape the course of development?

Man shares with other mammals – and with some non-mammalian species as well – a strong disposition to care for and rear young. Man differs from other species in the flexibility of his patterns of behaviour, a flexibility which extends to his patterns of child-rearing. Patterns of child-rearing differ widely from one society to another, and in Western societies have varied substantially from one century to another. Only since the beginning of the present century however, has child-rearing been influenced by psychological science. Within this brief period there have already been, under the impetus of theory, fact, and opinion, several wide swings of the pendulum of practice. Each swing has been multiply determined – by a new scientific position, by recognition of the ill-effects of previous practices, by indirect influence of other social changes, and by the simple fact that each new generation of parents is more influenced than it knows by a tendency to treat children in ways similar to those itself experienced. These things being so, it would be over-sanguine to hope that research projects now on the psychological drawing-boards will yield results that will soon lead to a great improvment in methods of child-rearing with consequent diminution of the world's ills. In the long run, nevertheless, such improvement is the hope implicit in all research arising from recognition of the ill-effects of maternal deprivation.

CONCLUSION

Conclusion

THE proper care of children deprived of a normal home life can now be seen to be not merely an act of common humanity, but to be essential for the mental and social welfare of a community. For, when their care is neglected, as still happens in every country of the Western world today, they grow up to reproduce themselves. Deprived children, whether in their own homes or out of them, are the source of social infection as real and serious as are carriers of diphtheria and typhoid. And, just as preventive measures have reduced these diseases to negligible proportions, so can determined action greatly reduce the number of deprived children in our midst and the growth of adults liable to produce more of them.

Yet, so far in no country is the problem being tackled on the necessary scale. Even in so-called advanced countries there is a tolerance for conditions of bad mental hygiene in nurseries, institutions, and hospitals to a degree which, if it were found in the field of physical hygiene, would long since have led to public outcry. The break-up of families and the shunting of illegitimates are accepted without comment. The twin problems of neglectful parents and deprived children are viewed as inevitable and left to reproduce themselves. It seems probable that the main reasons for this fatalism are three in number: the belief that a large proportion of these children are orphans and have no relatives; an economic system which from time to time creates unrelieved poverty on a scale so great that social workers are powerless to help; and a lack of understanding of psychiatric factors and a consequent powerlessness in managing cases where they are important. In many Western countries, however, these three conditions no longer hold, but two others remain which hinder progress. In the first place, there is still a woeful scarcity of social workers skilled in the ability to diagnose the presence of psychiatric factors and to deal with them effectively. From what has been said hitherto, it is evident that unless a social worker has a good understanding of unconscious motives she will be powerless to deal with many an unmarried mother, many a home which is in danger of breaking up, and many a case of conflict between parent and child. There is a tremendous task before all countries to train social workers in appropriate methods and child psychiatrists to aid them.

The second factor still at work is a lack of conviction on the part of governments, social agencies, and the public that mother-love in infancy and childhood is as important for mental health as are vitamins and proteins for physical health. This lack of conviction has two roots – emotional and intellectual. A strong prejudice against believing it is not infrequently found in people who get very heated about the alleged failure of children's own parents and who have a conspicuous need, of which they are not always aware, to prove themselves better able to look after the children than can their own parents. Members of committees, too, in contemplating the fruits of their labours, are apt to find more personal satisfaction in visiting an institution and reviewing a docile group of physically well-cared-for children than in trying to imagine the same children, rather more grubby perhaps, happily playing in their own or foster-homes. One must beware of a vested interest in the institutional care of children!

The intellectual doubts are more easily dealt with and may perhaps have been influenced by the scientific evidence reviewed in the first and third parts of this book.

To those whose duty it is to act against these evils, the present position may be likened to that facing their predecessors responsible for public health a century ago. Theirs was a great opportunity for ridding their countries of dirt-borne diseases; some took it, others remained critical of the evidence and did nothing. True, the evidence presented in this book is at many points faulty, many gaps remain unfilled, and critical information is often missing; but it must be remembered that evidence is never complete, that knowledge of truth is always partial, and that to await certainty is to await eternity. Let it be hoped, then, that all over the world men and women in public life will recognize the relation of mental health to maternal care, and will seize their opportunities for promoting courageous and far-reaching reforms.

List of Authorities referred to but not named

PARTS I–II

Where quotations are made full bibliographical details are given. In other cases (with one or two exceptions) details will be found in the full bibliography at the end of *Maternal Care and Mental Health.*

PAGE 15 Stott, D. H.
16 Hunt, J. McV.
Gregg, N. M.
17 Lorenz, K.
22 Bakwin, H.
23 Brodbeck, A. J., and Irwin, O. C.
Spitz, R. A., and Wolf, K. M.
24 Rheingold, H. L.
Levy, R. J.
Goldfarb, W.
Simonsen, K. M.
25 Liddell, H.
26 Daniels, E.
Bakwin, H. *American Journal of Diseases of Childhood*, **63**, 30 (1942).
28 Spitz, R. A., and Wolf, K. M.
29, 30, 31 Burlingham, D., Freud, A., and Hellman, I. *Monthly Report of Hampstead Nurseries* for May 1944 (unpublished).
Young Children in Wartime, London (1942).
Infants without Families, London (1943).
34 Edelston, H.
Isaacs, S.
36 Levy, D. *American Journal of Psychiatry*, **94**, 643 (1935).
38 Levy, D. (as above).
Powdermaker, F., Levis, H. T., and Touraine, G. *American Journal of Orthopsychiatry*, **7**, 58 (1937).
Lowrey, L. G. *American Journal of Orthopsychiatry*, **10**, 576 (1940).
Bender, L., and Yarnell, H. *American Journal of Psychiatry*, **97**, 1158 (1941).
39 Goldfarb, W. *Journal of Experimental Education*, **12**, 106 (1943).
Bowlby, J. *International Journal of Psychoanalysis*, **21**, 154 (1940).
40 Bender, J. *Handbook of Correctional Psychology*, ed. Lindner & Seliger, New York (1947).
41 Carey-Trefzer, C. J.

PAGE 42 Fitzgerald, O. *Journal of Mental Science*, **94**, 701 (1948).
Kemp, T. *Prostitutes: Their Early Lives*, League of Nations, Geneva (1938).
43 Goldfarb, W. *Journal of Experimental Education*, **12**, 106 (1943).
46 Theis, S. van S.
47 Orgel, S. Z.
Brown, F.
Bodman, F., MacKinlay, M., and Sykes, K.
48 Alt, H. *American Journal of Orthopsychiatry*, **21**, 105 (1951).
50 Brosse, T., and Meierhofer, M. *Homeless Children* (UNESCO), Paris (1950).
War Handicapped Children (UNESCO), Paris (1950).
Loosli-Usteri, M.
51 Szondi, L.
Tibout, N. H. C., and others.
51–2 Piquer y Jover, J. J. *El niño abandonado y delincuente*, Madrid (1946).
56 Levy, D. *American Journal of Psychiatry*, **94**, 643 (1937).
Powdermaker, F., and others.
58 Bender, L.
61–2 Corner, G. W. *Ourselves Unborn*, New Haven (1944).
79 Theis, S. van S.
Simonsen, K. M.
81 *Children and the British Government Evacuation Scheme*, Ministry of Health, London (1948).
Healy, W., Bronner, A. F., Baylor, E. M. H., and Murphy, J.P. *Reconstructing Behaviour in Youth*, New York (1929).
91 *The Neglected Child and his Family*, National Council of Social Service, Oxford (1948).
93 Querido, A.
95 Hopkirk, H. W.
95 Terman, L. M.
Burgess, E. W., and Cottrell, L. S., jnr.
97 Brill, K.
100 *The Placing of Children in Families*, League of Nations, Geneva (1938).
101 Baylor, E. M. H., and Monachesi, E. D. *The Rehabilitation of Children*, New York (1939).
103 Berkowitz, S. J.
104 Wilson, A. T. M. *Human Relations*, **2**, 233 (1949).
112 Young, L. R.
113 Young, L. R. In: *Understanding the Psychology of the Unmarried Mother*, Family Service Association of America, New York (1947).
114 Wittkower, E. D. *British Journal of Venereal Diseases*, **24**, 59 (1948).

PAGE 115 Safier, B., Corrigan, H. G., Fein, E. J., and Bradway, K. P. *A Psychiatric Approach to the Treatment of Promiscuity*, New York (1949).
116 *Annual Health Report* for 1939, Willesden, Middlesex.
119 Rome, R.
120 Embry, M. *Planning for the Unmarried Mother*, New York (1937).
Morlock, M., and Campbell, H. *Maternity Homes for Unmarried Mothers*, Washington, D.C. (1946).
127 Wolkonir, B.
129 Hutchinson, D. *In Quest of Foster Parents*, New York (1943).
137–8 Isaacs, S.
Cowan, E. A., and Stout, E.
140 Gordon, H. L. *Child Welfare*, **29**, January, p. 3 (1950).
141 Pollock, J. C., and Rose, J. A.
145 Baker, I. M. *Child Welfare*, **28**, May, p. 3 (1949).
146–7 Klein, M.
Burlingham, D., and Freud, A. *Annual Report of a Residential War Nursery*, London (1942).
148 Theis, S. van S.
149 Jolowicz, A. R. *The Hidden Parent*, New York State Conference of Social Welfare (1946).
153 Mulock Houwer, D. Q. R. *Enige aspecten der jeugdige politike delinquenten*, Amsterdam (1947).
157 Hopkirk, H. W.
Stern, E. M.
158 Bettelheim, B., and Sylvester, E.
160 Richman, L. H.
Mulock Houwer, D. Q. R.
162 Clothier, F.
Richman, L. H.
163 Murphy, L. B.
169–70 Winnicott, D. W., and Britton, C. 'The Problem of Homeless Children', in *Children's Communities*, London (New Education Fellowship Monograph, No. 1, p. 1).
171 Winnicott, D. W., and Britton, C.
Bettelheim, B., and Sylvester, E.
173 Winnicott, D. W., and Britton, C. *Human Relations*, **1**, 87 (1947).
174 Bettelheim, B., and Sylvester, E. *American Journal of Orthopsychiatry*, **18**, 191 (1948).
175–6 Spence, J. C. *British Medical Journal*, **1**, 125 (1947).
177–8 Pickerill, C., and H. P. *Nursing Mirror*, August (1947).
179 Spence, J. C. (see reference to p. 175–6).

References to Authorities

PART III

Where full bibliographical details are not given in the following notes, they will be found in the bibliography at the end of Dr Ainsworth's paper in the W H O publication, *Deprivation of Maternal Care*, Public Health Papers, No. 14, 1962.

PAGE 193 Mead, Margaret. 'A cultural anthropologist's approach to maternal deprivation', in: *Deprivation of Maternal Care: a Reassessment of its Effects*. Geneva, World Health Organization, *Public Health Papers*, No. 14, pp. 45–62 (1962).

196 Spitz, R. A., and Wolf, K. M. (1946).

196 Bender, L., and Yarnell, H. (1941).

198 Ainsworth, M. D., and Bowlby, J. (1954).

202 Prugh, D. G., and Harlow, R. G. ' "Masked deprivation" in infants and young children', in: *Deprivation of Maternal Care: a Reassessment of its Effects*. Geneva, World Health Organization, *Public Health Papers*, No. 14, pp. 9–30 (1962). Also, Coleman, R. W., and Provence, S. (1957).

202 Lewis, H. (1954).

202 Clarke, A. D. N., and Clarke, A. M. (1957, 1959, 1960); and Reiman, S. (1958).

202 e.g. Robertson, Joyce (1962).

206 David, M., and Appell, G. (1961, 1962).

206 Rheingold, H. L. (1956); Rheingold, H. L., and Bayley, N. (1959).

207 Gardner, D. B., Hawkes, G. R., and Burchinal, L. G. (1961).

207 Mead, Margaret, *op. cit.*

208 Burlingham, D., and Freud, A. (1944).

208 Harlow, H. F. (1958, 1960, 1961).

208 Ainsworth, Mary D. 'The development of infant-mother interaction among the Ganda', in: Foss, B. M. (Ed.), *Determinants of infant behaviour*, *II*, Methuen, London (1963).

210 Rabin, A. I. (1957, 1958, 1959); Spiro, M. E. (1955).

210 Schaffer, H. R., and Emerson, P. E. (1964); *The Development of Social Attachments in Infancy*, Child Development Monograph, No. 94.

210 Stolz, L. M. (1960).

211 Coleman, R. W., and Provence, S. (1957).

211 Siegel, A. E. (Ed.) (1961).

212 Spitz, R. A. (1945, 1946); Spitz, R. A., and Wolf, K. M. (1946).
212 Skeels, H. M., Updegraff, R., Wellman, B., and Williams, H. M. (1938); Skeels, H. M., and Dye, H. B. (1939).
212 McNemar, Q. (1940); Pinneau, S. R. (1955).
212 E.g. Roudinesco, J., and Appell, G. (1950, 1951).
212 Provence, S., and Lipton, R. C. *Infants in Institutions*, International Universities Press, New York (1962).
213 Robertson, J. (1953); and Bowlby, J. (1952); also Bowlby, J. (1953, 1954).
213 Bowlby, J. (1958–1961); and Bowlby, J. 'Pathological mourning and childhood mourning', in *Journal of American Psychoanalytic Association*, **11**, 500–541 (1963).
213 Jessner, L., Blom, G. E., and Waldfogel, S. (1952).
214 Prugh, D. G., Staub, E. M., Sands, J. H., Kirschbaum, R. M., and Lenihan, E. A. (1953).
214 Aubry, J. (1955); David, M., Nicholas, H., and Roudinesco, J. (1952).
214 Heinicke, C. M. (1956).
214 Schaffer, H. R. (1958); Schaffer, H. R., and Callender, W. M. (1959).
214 Yarrow, L. J. 'Research in dimensions of early maternal care', in *Merrill-Palmer Quarterly*, **9**, 101–114 (1963).
215 Beres, D., and Obers, S. J. (1950).
215 Goldfarb, W. (1947).
216 Bowlby, J., Ainsworth, M. D., Boston, M., and Rosenbluth, D. (1956).
216 Stott, D. H. (1956).
216 Earle, A. M., and Earle, B. V. (1961).
216 Earle, A. M., and Earle, B. V. (1961); Barry, H. (1949); Barry, H. and Lindemann, E. (1960); Brown, F. (1961).
217 Bowlby, J. (1960b, 1961a, 1961b, 1963).
217 Trasler, G. (1960).
218 Pringle, M. L. Kellmer, and Bossio, V. (1960).
221 e.g. Dennis, W. and Najarian, P. (1957).
221 e.g. Lewis, H. (1954).
221 e.g. David, M., and Appell, G. (1951); Alpert, A. 'A special therapeutic technique for certain developmental disorders in prelatency children', in *American Journal of Orthopsychiatry*, **27**, 256–270 (1957).
221 Robertson, J. (1953); Robertson, J., and Bowlby, J. (1952).
223 Riesen, A. H. 'Arrested vision', in *Scientific American*, **183**, 16–19 (1950). Riesen, A. H. 'Effects of stimulus deprivation on the development and atrophy of the visual sensory system', in *American Journal of Orthopsychiatry* **30**, 23–26 (1960). Rasch, E., Swift, H., Riesen, A. H., and

Chow, K. L. 'Altered structure and composition of retinal cells in dark-reared mammals', in *Experimental Cell Research*, **25**, 348–363 (1961).
223 A good review and discussion of the evidence in regard to intellectual development is given by Hunt, J. McV., in *Intelligence and Experience*, Ronald Press, New York (1961).
224 Robertson, J. (1953); Jessner, L., Blom, G. E., and Waldfogel, S. (1952); Jackson, K., Winkley, R., Faust, O. A., and Cermak, E. G. (1952); Heinicke, C. M. (1956).
224 e.g. Skeels, H. M., and Harms, I. (1948); Skodak, M., and Skeels, H. M. (1949); Skeels, H. M., and Dye, H. B. (1939); Fischer, L. L. (1952).
224 e.g. Rheingold, H., and Bayley, N. (1959).
224 Goldfarb, W., especially (1943b).
224 Bowlby, J., Ainsworth, M. D., Boston, M., and Rosenbluth, D. (1956).
225 Personal communication.
225 Spitz, R. A., and Wolf, K. M. (1946); Schaffer, H. R., and Callender, W. M. (1959); Yarrow, L. M. (1963) in 'Research in dimensions of early maternal care', in *op. cit.*
227 e.g. Douglas, J. W. B., and Blomfield, J. M. (1958); Rowntree, G. (1955); Gardner, D. B., Hawkes, G. R., and Burchinal, L. G. (1961).
228 Wardle, C. J. (1961).
229 Glueck, S., and Glueck, E. T. (1950).
229 Andry, R. G. 'Paternal and maternal roles and delinquency', in *Deprivation of Maternal Care: a Reassessment of its Effects*. Geneva: World Health Organization, *Public Health Papers*, No. 14, pp. 31–44 (1962).
229 Naess, S. (1959); Naess, S. 'Mother separation and delinquency: further evidence', in *British Journal of Criminology*, **2**, 361–374 (1962).
229 e.g. Bowlby, J., Ainsworth, M. D., Boston, M., and Rosenbluth, D. (1956); Stott, D. H. (1956); and also Goldfarb, W., especially (1943b).
230 Cf. Andry, R. G. (1962), *op. cit.*
231 e.g. Casler, L. 'Maternal Deprivation: a Critical Review of the Literature', in *Monog. Soc. Res. Child Development*, 26, No. 2, 1–64 (1961).
231 Yarrow, L. J. (1961).
231 Schaffer, H. R., and Emerson, P. E., *op. cit.*
232 Skeels, H. M., Updegraff, R., Wellman, B., and Williams, H. M. (1938); Skeels, H. M., and Harms, I. (1948); Skeels, H. M., and Dye, H. B. (1939).
233 Bakwin, H. (1942–49).

233 Hunt, J. McV. *op. cit.*
233 Piaget, J. *The Origins of Intelligence in Children*, International Universities Press, New York (1952); *The Construction of Reality in the Child*, Basic Books, New York (1954)

Index

On account of closely limited space similar though not identical subjects are grouped under a general heading, e.g. 'Workers'. Names of towns outside the U.K. are omitted; references to them will be found under the name of their country.

Index

Index

The World Health Organization

The World Health Organization (WHO) is a specialized agency of the United Nations and represents the culmination of efforts to establish a single inter-governmental health agency. As such, it inherits the functions of antecedent organizations such as the Office International d'Hygiène Publique, the Health Organization of the League of Nations, and the Health Division of UNRRA.

WHO had its origin in the proposal made at the United Nations Conference held in San Francisco in 1945 that a specialized agency be created to deal with all matters relating to health. In 1946, representatives of sixty-one governments met at the International Health Conference, New York, drafted and signed the WHO Constitution, and established an Interim Commission to serve until the Constitution could be ratified by twenty-six Member States of the United Nations. The Constitution came into force on 7 April 1948, the first World Health Assembly met in Geneva in June 1948, and on 1 September 1948, the permanent Organization was established.

The work of the Organization is carried out by three organs: the World Health Assembly, the supreme authority, to which all Member States send delegates; the Executive Board, the executive organ of the Health Assembly, consisting of eighteen persons designated by as many Member States; and a Secretariat under the Director-General.

The scope of WHO's interests and activities exceeds that of any previous international health organization and includes programmes relating to a wide variety of public health questions: malaria, tuberculosis, venereal diseases, other communicable diseases, maternal and child health, mental health, social and occupational health, nutrition, nursing, environmental sanitation, public health administration, professional education and training, and health education of the public. In addition, WHO undertakes or participates in certain technical work of international significance, such as the compilation of an international pharmacopoeia, the setting up of biological standards and of standards for insecticides and insecticide-spraying apparatus, the control of addiction-producing drugs, the exchange of scientific information, the drawing up of international sanitary regulations, the revision of the international list of diseases and causes of death, the collection and dissemination of epidemiological information, and statistical studies on morbidity and mortality.